OBSERVATIONS

ON

MADNESS

AND

MELANCHOLY:

INCLUDING

PRACTICAL REMARKS ON THOSE DISEASES;

TOGETHER WITH

CASES:

AND AN

ACCOUNT OF THE MORBID APPEARANCES

ON

DISSECTION.

By

JOHN HASLAM

"Of the uncertainties of our present state, the most dreadful
and alarming is the uncertain continuance of reason."
Dr. Johnson's Rasselas.

AS
A GRATEFUL ACKNOWLEDGMENT
FOR MANY FAVOURS,
AN OBLATION TO SUBSISTING FRIENDSHIP,
AND A
TRIBUTE TO SUPERIOR JUDGMENT,
EXERCISING THE PROFESSION OF MEDICINE WITH
SKILL AND LIBERALITY:
THE PRESENT VOLUME IS RESPECTFULLY
DEDICATED TO
DR. THOMAS MONRO,
A FELLOW OF THE COLLEGE, AND PHYSICIAN
TO BETHLEM HOSPITAL.

PREFACE.

THE alarming increase of Insanity, as might naturally be expected, has incited many persons to an investigation of this disease;—some for the advancement of Science, and others with the hope of emolument.

More than ten years having elapsed since the publication of the "Observations on Insanity," a trifle, which the Profession has held in greater estimation than its intrinsic merits could justify: the present work is modestly introduced to the public notice, as a corrected copy of the former, with considerable additions, which the extensive scope of Bethlem Hospital would have furnished more liberally to a more intelligent observer.

To have taken a comprehensive survey of the human faculties in their sound state; to have exhibited them impaired by natural decay, and transformed by disease, would have implied an ability to which I cannot pretend; would have required many volumes to unfold, and perhaps more patience than any rational experience could have attributed to the reader. The contents of the following pages are therefore to be considered as an abbreviated relation, and condensed display of many years observation and practice, in a situation affording constant opportunities and abundant supplies for such investigations.

It is natural to presume, that amongst my professional acquaintance the subject of Insanity must have been frequently introduced as a topic of discourse; and I am ready to acknowledge, that I have often profited by their remarks and suggestions: but I should be ungrateful were I not to confess my particular obligations to my esteemed friend,

Anthony Carlisle, Esq. Surgeon to the Westminster Hospital, for many corrections, and some communications, which I shall ever value as judicious and important.

Bethlem Hospital,
Nov. 21, 1808.

CHAPTER I.

DEFINITION.

THERE is no word in the English language more deserving of a precise definition than madness: and if those who have treated on this subject have been so unfortunate as to disagree with each other, and consequently have left their readers to reconcile their discordant opinions; yet it must be confessed that considerable pains have been bestowed, to convey a clear and accurate explanation of this term. Although this contrariety of sentiment has prevailed concerning the precise meaning of the word madness, medical practitioners have been sufficiently reconciled as to the thing itself: so that when they have seen an insane person, however opposite their definitions, they have readily coincided that the patient was mad.

From this it would appear that the thing itself, is, generally speaking, sufficiently plain and intelligible; but that the term which represents the thing is obscure. Perhaps, we might be somewhat assisted, by tracing back this word, in order to discover its original meaning, and shewing from its import the cause of its imposition.

If the reader, as is now the custom, should turn to Johnson's Dictionary for the meaning and etymology of this word, he will find that the Doctor has derived it both from the Anglo-Saxon ʒemaað and the Italian *matto*; but without giving any meaning as the cause of its employment. The word is originally Gothic, and meant anger, rage, 𐌌𐍉𐌳. [Mod]. It is true that we have now converted the o, into a, and write the word mad: but mod was anciently employed.

"Yet sawe I MODNESSE laghyng in his *rage*."
Chaucer. Knight's Tale, fol. 1561, *p.* 6.

There is so great a resemblance between anger and violent madness, that there is nothing which could more probably have led to the adoption of the term. Dr. Beddoes, who appears to have examined the subject of insanity with the eye of an enlightened philosopher, is decidedly of this opinion, he says, Hygeia, *No.* 12, *p.* 40, "Mad, is one of those words which mean almost every thing and nothing. At first, it was, I imagine, applied to the transports of rage; and when men were civilized enough to be capable of insanity, their insanity, I presume, must have been of the frantic sort, because in the untutored, intense feelings seem regularly to carry a boisterous expression."

Mad is therefore not a complex idea, as has been supposed, but a complex term for all the forms and varieties of this disease. Our language has been enriched with other terms expressive of this affection, all of which have a precise meaning. Delirium, which we have borrowed from the latin, merely means, *out of the track*, de lira, so that a delirious person, one who starts out of the track regularly pursued, becomes compared to the same deviation in the process of ploughing. *Crazy*, we have borrowed from the French *ecrasé*, crushed, broken: we still use the same meaning, and say that such a person is crack'd. Insane, deranged, or disarranged,[1] melancholic, out of one's wits, lunatic, phrenetic, or as we have corrupted it, frantick, require no explanation. *Beside one's self* most probably originated from the belief of possession by a devil, or evil spirit.

The importance of investigating the original meaning of words must be evident when it is considered that the law of this country impowers persons of the medical profession to confine and discipline those to whom the term mad or lunatic can fairly be applied. Instead of endeavouring to discover an infallible definition of madness, which I believe will be found impossible, as it is an attempt to comprise, in a few words, the wide range and mutable character of this Proteus disorder: much more advantage would be obtained if the circumstances could be precisely defined under which it is justifiable to deprive a human being of his liberty.

Another impediment to an accurate definition of madness, arises from the various hypotheses, which have been entertained concerning the powers and operations of the human mind: and likewise from the looseness and unsettled state of the terms by which it is to be defined.

Before treating of the intellect in a deranged state, it will perhaps be expected that some system of the human mind, in its perfect and healthy condition, should be laid down. It will be supposed necessary to establish in what sanity of intellect consists, and to mark distinctly some fixed point, the aberrations from which are to constitute disease.

To have a thorough knowledge of the nature, extent, and rectitude of the human faculties, is particularly incumbent on him who undertakes to write of them in their distempered state; and, in a legal point of view, it is most important that the medical practitioner should be enabled to establish the state of the patient's case, as a departure from that which *is* reason.

The difficulty of proposing a satisfactory theory of the human mind, must have been felt by every person, who has touched this delicate string since the days of Aristotle, and failure must be expected in him who attempts it: yet the endeavour is laudable, and miscarriage is not linked with disgrace. Every contribution, to illustrate what are the powers of mind we possess; how we are acted upon by external circumstances in the acquisition of knowledge; and concerning the manner in which we use this knowledge for the purposes of life; ought to be candidly received.

Enquiries of this nature have been usually conducted by commenting on the numerous and discordant authorities which have treated on metaphysical subjects; these persons, however they may differ on many points, appear to be pretty generally agreed, that the human mind possesses certain faculties and powers; as imagination, judgment, reason, and memory. They seem to consider these, as so many departments, or offices of the mind, and therefore class men according to the excellence or predominance of these powers. One man, is said to be distinguished by the brilliancy of his imagination; another, by the solidity of his judgment; a third, by the acuteness of his reason; and a fourth, by the promptitude and accuracy of his recollection.

As far as I have observed respecting the human mind, (and I speak with great hesitation and diffidence,) it does not possess, all those powers and faculties with which the pride of man has thought proper to invest it. By our senses, we are enabled to become acquainted with objects, and we are capable of recollecting them in a greater or less degree; the rest, appears to be merely a contrivance of language.

If mind, were actually capable of the operations attributed to it, and possessed of these powers, it would necessarily have been able to create a language expressive of these powers and operations. But the fact is otherwise. The language, which characterizes mind and its operations, has been borrowed from external objects; for mind has no language peculiar to itself. A few instances will sufficiently illustrate this position. After having committed an offence it is natural to say that the mind feels contrition and sorrow.

Contrition is from *cum* and *tero*, to rub together, which cannot possibly have any thing to do with the operations of the mind, which is incapable of rubbing its ideas or notions together. Contrition is a figurative expression, and may possibly mean the act of rubbing out the stain of vice, or wearing down by friction the prominences of sin.

If we were to analyze the word Sorrow, which is held to be a mental feeling, we should find it to be transferred from bodily sufferance: for the mind, is incapable of creating a term correctly expressive of its state, and therefore, it became necessary to borrow it from *soreness* of body.—*See Mr. Tooke's Diversions of Purley, vol.* ii. *p.* 207, where *sore, sorry,* and *sorrow* are clearly made out to be the same word.

It is customary to speak of a man, of accurate perceptions, and of another, who has grand and luminous conceptions of human nature. Perception, from *per*, and *capio* to take, seize, grasp, through the medium of the organs of sense, being implied. But to take, seize, and grasp are the operations of the hand, and can only, by extreme courtesy, be attributed to mind.

Mr. Dugald Stewart, the most thoughtful and intelligent of modern metaphysicians, has said, "By conception I mean that power of the mind which enables it to form a notion of an absent object of perception, or of a sensation which it has formerly felt."—*Elements of the Philosophy of the Human Mind,* 8vo. *p.* 133.

This definition means merely memory; and by perusing attentively the whole chapter the reader will be convinced of it. Conception, from *cum* and *capio*, has been applied to mind from the physical sense of embracing, comprehending, or probably from the notion of being impregnated with the subject. It may be remarked, that these three terms, by which conception has been explained, have been all applied to mental operation.

The words reason and reasoning, I believe, in most languages, strictly imply numeration, reckoning, proportion; the Latin *ratio, ratiocinor, ratiocinator* are sufficient examples. A curious coincidence between the Latin *ratio* and the Gothic *rathjo*, together with some pertinent and interesting observations, may be seen in Ihre's Glossarium Svio-gothicum, *p.* 393, *art.* Rækna. As we now acknowledge the science of number to be the purest system of reasoning, a system, on which all persons agree, and so unlike medicine, politics, and divinity, concerning which there is a constant, and hostile variety of sentiment, it adds some force to the argument. Indeed, Mr. Locke, who almost personifies reason, after having painfully sifted this matter, appears to be much of the same way of thinking: he says, "Reason, though it penetrates into the depth of the sea and earth, elevates our thoughts as high as the stars, and leads us through the vast spaces and large rooms of this mighty fabrick, *yet it comes far short of the real extent of even corporeal being*; and there are many instances wherein it fails us: as,

"First: it perfectly fails us where our ideas fail: it neither does, nor can extend itself farther than they do, and therefore, wherever we have no ideas our reasoning stops, and we are at an end of our reckoning: and if at any time *we reason about words, which do not stand for any ideas*, it is only about those sounds, and nothing else.

"Secondly: our reason is often puzzled, and at a loss, because of the obscurity, confusion or imperfection of the ideas it is employed about; and there we are involved in difficulties and contradictions. Thus, not having any perfect idea of the least extension of matter, nor of infinity, we are at a loss about the divisibility of matter; *but having perfect, clear, and distinct ideas of number, our reason meets with none of those inextricable difficulties in numbers, nor finds itself involved in any contradictions about them."—Works. 4to, vol. i, p.* 431.

It can scarcely be necessary, longer to fatigue the patience of the reader, by reverting to the etymology of those terms, which have been considered as significant of mind and its operations. Every one will be able sufficiently to develope imagination, reflection, combination, [as applied to ideas, importing the amalgamation of *two* into one] abstraction, [*vide Mr. Tooke, from p.* 15 to 426, *vol.* ii.] and a variety of others; and to shew, that they have arisen from physical objects, and the circumstances which surround us, and are independant of any operation which mind has elaborated.

But as madness, by some, has been exclusively held to be a disease of the imagination, and by others, to be a defect of the judgment; considering these as separate and independant powers or faculties of the intellect; it is certainly worth the trouble to enquire, whether such states of mind did ever exist as original and unconnected disorders. With respect to imagination, there can be but little difficulty; yet this will so far involve the judgment and memory, that it will not be easy to institute a distinction. If a cobbler should suppose himself an emperor, this supposition, may be termed an elevated flight, or an extensive stretch of imagination, but it is likewise a great defect in his judgment, to deem himself that which he is not, and it is certainly an equal lapse of his recollection, to forget what he really is.

Having endeavoured to give some reasons for not according with the generally received opinions, concerning the different powers of the mind, it may be proper shortly to state, that, from the manner in which we acquire knowledge, the human mind appears to be composed of a sum of individual perceptions: that, in proportion as we dwell by the eye, the ear, or the touch on any object (which is called attention,) we are more likely to become acquainted with it, and to be able to remember it. For the most part, we remember these perceptions in the succession in which they were presented, although, they may afterwards, from circumstances, be differently sorted.

The minds of ordinary men are well contented to deal out their ideas, in the order in which they were received; and, not having found the necessity of bringing them to bear on general subjects, they are commonly minutely accurate in the detail of that which they have observed. By such persons, a story is told with all the relations of time and place; connected with the persons who were present, their situation, state of health, and a vast variety of associated particulars; and these persons, however tedious, generally afford the most correct account. On the other hand, those who are men of business, and have much to communicate in a given space, are obliged to subtract the more material circumstances from the gross narrative, and exhibit these as the sum total. It is in this way, that words, originally of considerable length, have been abbreviated for the conveniency of dispatch, and from this necessity short hand writing has been employed.

As the science of arithmetic consists in addition to, or subtraction from, a given number; so does the human mind appear to be capable solely of adding to, or separating from, its stock of ideas, as pleasure may prompt, or necessity enforce.

Language, the representative of thought, bears the same construction; and it is curious to remark in the investigation of its abbreviations, that those words, which serve to connect ideas together, (*conjunctions*) and which have been supposed to mark certain operations of intellect, postures of mind, and turns of thought, have merely the force and meaning of to add, or to subtract.

Insanity is now generally divided into Mania and Melancholia, but formerly its distributions were more numerous. Paracelsus, speaking of this disease, says, "Vesaniæ hujus genera quatuor existunt: primi *Lunatici* vocantur: secundi *Insani*: tertii *Vesani*: quarti *Melancholici*, Lunatici sunt qui omnem suum morbum ex Luna accipiunt, et juxta eam sese gerunt ac moventur. Insani sunt, qui malum id ab utero materno hauserunt, veluti hæreditarium, uno subindè insaniam in alterum transferente. Vesani sunt, qui a cibis ac potibus ita inficiuntur ac taminantur, ut ratione sensuque priventur. Melancholici sunt, qui ex intimæ naturæ vitio a ratione deturbantur, et ad vesaniam precipitantur." Paracelsus, however, thinks that a fifth genus may be added. "Ad quatuor hac genera genus insuper aliud quodammodo annumerari potest, videlicet *obsessi*, qui a diabolo variis modis occupari solent."—*Paracelsi Opera, folio, tom.* i. *fol.* 572.

The idea of being besieged, beset, or possessed by the devil was formerly a very favourite notion, and is derived to us by an authority we are taught to reverence: indeed it is still the opinion of many harmless and believing persons, some of whom have bestowed considerable pains to convince me that the violent and mischievous maniacs in Bedlam were under the dominion of this insinuating spirit. They have employed one argument which would seem to have considerable weight, namely, that the most atrocious crimes are stated in our indictments (much to the credit of human nature) to have been committed by the instigation of the devil: and they have also endeavoured to explain, how a late and eminently successful practitioner, by an union of the holy office with consummate medical skill, was enabled to cure nine lunatics out of ten, which certainly has not hitherto been accounted for.

Paracelsus, who contemplated this subject with uncommon gravity and solicitude, is of opinion that the devil enters us much in the same manner as a maggot gets into a filbert.— *Vide Fragmentum Libri Philosophiæ de Dæmoniacis et Obsessis, tom.* ii. *p.* 460.

To conclude this part of the subject, and to exhibit the state of belief at that period, I shall take the liberty of extracting a portion from the 11th chapter of Dr. Andrewe Boord's Extravagantes, which "doth shewe of a Demoniacke person, the which is possessed of or with the devyll or devylls.

"Demoniacus or Demoniaci be the Latin wordes. In Greke it is named Demonici. In Englyshe it is named he or they, the whiche be mad and possessed of the devyll or devils, and their propertie is to hurt and kyll them selfe, or els to hurt and kyll any other thynge, therfore let every man beware of them, and kepe them in a sure custody.

The cause of this Matter.

"This matter doth passe all maner sickenesses and diseases, and it is a fearefull and terryble thyng to se a devyll or devylles shoulde have so muche and so greate a power over man, as it is specified of such persons dyvers tymes in the gospell, specyally in the IX. Chapitre of St. Marke. Chryste sendynge his disciples to preache the worde of God, gevynge them power to make sicke men whole, lame men to go, blynde to se, &c. Some of them dyd go by a mans that was possessed of devils and they coud not make him whole. Shortly to conclude, Chryst dyd make hym whole. The dysciples of Chryste asked of him why that they coud not make the possessed man of the devylls whole. And Jesus

Chryste said to them: this kynde of devylls can not be cast out without prayer and fastynge. Here it is to be noted, that nowe a dayes fewe or els none doth set by prayer or fastynge, regardyng not gods wordes; in this matter, I do feare that suche persons be possessed of the devil, although they be not starke madde, and to shew further of demoniacke persons the whiche be starke madde. The fyrste tyme that I dyd dwell in Rome, there was a gentilwoman of Germani, the whych was possessed of devyls, and she was brought to Rome to be made whole. For within the precynct of St. Peters church, without St. Peters chapel, standeth a pyller of whyte marble grated round about with iron, to the which our Lorde Jesus Chryste dyd lye in hymselfe unto the Pylates hal, as the Romaynes doth say, to the which pyller al those that be possessed of the devyl, out of dyvers countreys and nacions be brought thyther, and as they say of Rome, such persons be made there whole. Amonge al other this woman of Germany, which is CCCC myles and odde from Rome, was brought to the pyller, (I then there beyng presente,) with great strength and violently with a XX or mo men, this woman was put into that pyller within the yron grate, and after her dyd go in a preeste, and dyd examine the woman under this maner in the Italian tonge. Thou devyl or devyls, I do abjure thee by the potencial power of the father, and of the sonne our Lorde Jesus Christe, and by the vertue of the Holy Ghoste, that thou do shewe to me, for what cause that thou doeste possess this woman: what wordes was aunswered I will not write, for men will not beleve it, but wolde say it were a foule and great lye, but I dyd heare that I was afrayd to tarry any longer, lest that the devyls shulde have come out of her, and to have entred into me; remembrynge what is specified in the viii Chapitre of St. Matthewe, when that Jesus Christ had made two men whole, the whiche, was possessed with a legion of devils. A legion is IX M. IX C. nynety and nyne:

the sayd devyls dyd desyre Jesus, that when they were expelled out of the aforesayde twoo men, that they might enter into a herde of hogges, and so they did, and the hogges did runne into the sea and were drowned. I consyderynge this, and weke of faith and afeard, crossed myselfe and durste not heare and se such matters, for it was to stupendious and above all reason yf I shulde wryte it; and in this matter I dyd marvell of an other thynge; if the efficacitie of such makynge one whole, dyd rest in the vertue that was in the pyller, or els in the wordes that the preest dyd speake. I do judge it shulde be in the holy wordes that the prest dyd speak, and not in the pyller; for and yf it were in the pyller, the Byshops, and the Cardinalles that hathe ben many yeres past, and those that were in my tyme, and they that hath bin sence, wolde have had it in more reverence, and not to suffre rayne, hayle, snowe, and such wether to fal on it, for it hath no coverynge, but at laste when that I did consyder that the vernacle, the phisnomy of Christ, and scarse the sacrament of the aulter was in maner uncovered and al St. Peters Churche downe in ruyne, and utterly decayed, and nothing set by, consideringe in olde chapels, beggers and baudes, hoores and theves dyd lye within them, asses and moyles dyd defyle within the precincte of the Churche, and byenge and sellynge there was used within the precinct of the sayde church that it dyd pytie my harte and mynde to come and se any tyme more the sayde place and churche."—*Andrewe Boorde,*[2] *the seconde Boke of the Brevyary of health*, 1557, *fol. 4th.*

To return from this digression. Dr. Ferriar, whom to mention otherwise than as a man of genius, of learning, and of taste, would be unjust, has adopted the generally accepted division of insanity into mania and melancholia. In mania he conceives "false perception, and consequently confusion of ideas, to be a leading circumstance." The latter, he supposes to consist "in intensity of idea, which is a contrary state to false perception." From the observations I have been able to make respecting Mania, I have by no means been led to conclude, that false perception, is a leading circumstance in this disorder, and still less, that confusion of ideas must be the necessary consequence of false perception.

By perception I understand, with Mr. Locke, the apprehension[3] of sensations; and after a very diligent enquiry of patients who have recovered from the disease, and from an attentive observation of those labouring under it, I have not frequently found, that insane people perceive falsely the objects which have been presented to them.

We find madmen equally deranged upon those ideas, which they have been long in the possession of, and on which the perception has not been recently exercised, as respecting those, which they have lately received: and we frequently find those who become suddenly mad, talk incoherently upon every subject, and consequently, upon many, on which the perception has not been exercised for a considerable time.

It is well known, that maniacs often suppose they have seen and heard those things, which really did not exist at the time; but even this I should not explain by any disability, or error of the perception; since it is by no means the province of the perception to represent unreal existences to the mind. It must therefore be sought elsewhere; most probably in the senses.

We sometimes (more especially in the early stages of furious madness) find patients from very slight resemblances, and sometimes, where none whatever can be perceived by others of sound mind, confounding one person with another. Even in this case it does not seem necessary to recur to false perception for the explanation. It is equally probable that the organs of vision are affected in consequence of the disease of the brain, and therefore receive incorrect sensations: and still more likely, from the *rapid succession* in which objects are noticed, that a very slight trait of countenance would recal the idea [or name] of some particular person.

I have known many cases of patients who insisted that they had seen the devil. It might be urged, that in these instances, the perception was vitiated; but it must be observed there could be no perception of that, which was not present and existing at the time. Upon desiring these patients to describe what they had seen, they all represented him as a big, black man, with a long tail, and sharp talons, such as is seen pictured in books; a proof that the idea was revived in the mind from some former impressions. One of these patients however carried the matter a little further, as she solemnly declared, she heard him break the iron chain with which God had confined him, and saw him pass fleetly by her window, with a truss of straw upon his shoulder.

That "confusion of ideas" should be the necessary consequence of false perception, is very difficult to admit. It has often been observed that madmen will reason correctly from false premises, and the observation is certainly true: we have indeed occasion to notice the same thing in those of the soundest minds. It is very possible for the perception to be deceived in the occurrence of a thing, which, although it did not actually happen, yet was likely to take place; and which had frequently occurred before.—The reception of this as a truth, if the person were capable of deducing from it the proper inferences, could neither create confusion nor irregularity of ideas.

Melancholia, the other form in which this disease is supposed to exist, is made by Dr. Ferriar to consist in "intensity of idea." By intensity of idea, I presume is meant, that the mind is more strongly fixed on, or more frequently recurs to, a certain set of ideas, than when it is in a healthy state. But this definition applies equally to mania; for we every day see the most furious maniacs suddenly sink into a profound melancholia, and the most depressed and miserable objects become violent and raving. There are patients in Bethlem Hospital, whose lives are divided between furious and melancholic paroxysms, and who, under both forms, retain the same set of ideas. It must also have been observed, by those who are conversant with this disorder, that there is an intermediate state, which cannot be termed maniacal nor melancholic: a state of complete insanity, yet unaccompanied by furious or depressing passions.[4]

In speaking of the two forms of this disease, mania and melancholia, there is a circumstance sufficiently obvious, which hitherto does not appear to have been noticed: I mean the rapid or slow succession of the patient's ideas. Probably sound and vigorous mind consists as much in the moderate succession of our ideas, as in any other circumstance. It may be enquired, how we are to ascertain this increased, proportionate, and deficient activity of mind? From language, the medium by which thought is conveyed. The connexion between thought and utterance is so strongly cemented by habit, that the latter becomes the representative of the former.

The physiology of mind, I humbly conceive to be at present in its infancy, but there seems good reason to imagine, that furious madness implies a rapid succession of ideas; and the circumstance of rage, from whence its origin has been deduced, points out the hurried consecution. In this state of mind the utterance succeeds

—————————————————"sudden as the spark
From smitten steel; from nitrous grain the blaze."

and it frequently happens, after the tumult has subsided, the person remembers but little of that which had escaped him.

"I then, all-smarting with my wounds, being cold,
(To be so pestered with a popingay)
Out of my greefe, and my Impatience,
Answered (neglectingly) *I know not what—*
He should, or should not: for he made me *mad*."

From this connexion between thought and utterance, we find many persons (particularly those who are insane) talking to themselves; especially when their minds are intently occupied; and taking the converse, we frequently observe those who are desirous to acquire any subject by heart, repeating it aloud.

From the same cause we have often occasion to remark, that strong, and perhaps involuntary, propensity to repeat the emphatical words in a sentence, and which are commonly the last, before we endeavour to reply to, or confute them.

"*King.* No: on the barren Mountaine let him sterve:
For I shall never hold that man my friend
Whose tongue shall aske me for one peny cost
To ransome home revolted Mortimer.

"*Hotsp.* Revolted Mortimer?
He never did fall off, my Soveraigne Liege,
But by the chance of warre:"

As the terms Mania and Melancholia, are in general use, and serve to distinguish the forms under which insanity is exhibited, there can be no objection to retain them; but I would strongly oppose their being considered as opposite diseases. In both there is an equal derangement. On dissection, the state of the brain does not shew any appearances peculiar to melancholia; nor is the treatment, which I have observed most successful, different from that which is employed in mania.

As the practitioner's own mind must be the criterion, by which he infers the insanity of any other person; and when we consider the various, and frequently opposite, opinions of these intellectual arbitrators; the reader will be aware that I have not abstained from giving a definition of madness without some reason. There is indeed a double difficulty: the definition ought to comprize the aberrations of the lunatic, and fix the standard for the practitioner.

But it may be assumed that sound mind and insanity stand in the same predicament, and are opposed to each other in the same manner, as right to wrong, and as truth to the lie. In a general view no mistake can arise, and where particular instances create embarrassment, those most conversant with such persons will be best able to determine.

The terms sound mind and insanity are sufficiently plain. If to an ordinary observer, a person were to talk in an incoherent manner, he would think him mad; if his conduct were regular, and his observations pertinent, he would pronounce him in his senses: the two opposite states, well marked, are well understood; but there are many different shades, which are not so likely to strike the common examiner.

CHAP. II.

SYMPTOMS OF THE DISEASE.

ON this part of the subject, authors have commonly descended to minute particularities, and studied discriminations. Distinctions have been created, rather from the peculiar turn of the patient's propensities and discourse, than from any marked difference in the varieties and species of the disorder. Every person of sound mind, possesses something peculiar to himself, which distinguishes him from others, and constitutes his idiosyncrasy of body and individuality of character: in the same manner, every lunatic discovers something singular in his aberrations from sanity of intellect. It is not my intention to record these splintered subdivisions, but to exhibit the prominent features, by which insanity may be detected, as far as such appearances seem worthy of remark, and have been the subject of my own observation.

In most public hospitals, the first attack of diseases is seldom to be observed; and it might naturally be supposed, that there existed in Bethlem, similar impediments to an accurate knowledge of incipient madness. It is true, that all who are admitted into it, have been a greater, or less time afflicted with the disorder; yet from the occasional relapses to which insane persons are subject, we have frequent and sufficient opportunities of observing the beginning, and tracing the progress of this disease.

Among the incurables, there are some, who have intervals of perfect soundness of mind; but who are subject to relapses, which would render it improper, and even dangerous, to trust them at large in society: and with those, who are upon the curable establishment, a recurrence of the malady very frequently takes place. Upon these occasions, there is an ample scope for observing the first attack of the disease.

On the approach of mania, they first become uneasy,[5] are incapable of confining their attention, and neglect any employment to which they have been accustomed; they get but little sleep, they are loquacious, and disposed to harangue, and decide promptly, and positively upon every subject that may be started. Soon after, they are divested of all restraint in the declaration of their opinions of those, with whom they are acquainted. Their friendships are expressed with fervency and extravagance; their enmities with intolerance and disgust. They now become impatient of contradiction, and scorn reproof. For supposed injuries, they are inclined to quarrel and fight with those about them. They have all the appearance of persons inebriated, and those who are unacquainted with the symptoms of approaching mania, generally suppose them to be in a state of intoxication. At length suspicion creeps in upon the mind, they are aware of plots, which had never been contrived, and detect motives that were never entertained. At last the succession of ideas is too rapid to be examined;[6] the mind becomes crouded with thoughts, and confusion ensues.

Those under the influence of the depressing passions, will exhibit a different train of symptoms. The countenance wears an anxious and gloomy aspect, and they are little disposed to speak. They retire from the company of those with whom they had formerly associated, seclude themselves in obscure places, or lie in bed the greatest part of their time. Frequently they will keep their eyes fixed to some object for hours together, or continue them an equal time "bent on vacuity." They next become fearful, and conceive a thousand fancies:

often recur to some immoral act which they have committed, or imagine themselves guilty of crimes which they never perpetrated: believe that God has abandoned them, and, with trembling, await his punishment. Frequently they become desperate, and endeavour by their own hands to terminate an existence, which appears to be an afflicting and hateful incumbrance.

Madmen, do not always continue in the same furious or depressed states: the maniacal paroxysm abates of its violence, and some beams of hope, occasionally cheer the despondency of the melancholic patients. We have in the hospital some unfortunate persons, who are obliged to be secured the greater part of their time, but who now and then become calm, and to a certain degree rational: upon such occasions, they are allowed a greater range, and are admitted to associate with the others. In some instances the degree of rationality is more considerable; they conduct themselves with propriety, and in a short conversation will appear sensible and coherent. Such remission has been generally termed a *lucid interval*.

When medical persons are called upon to attend a commission of lunacy, they are always asked, whether the patient has had a *lucid interval*? A term of such latitude as interval, requires to be explained in the most perspicuous and accurate manner. [The circumstances which probably occasioned the employment of this term are pointed out in the chapter which enumerates the causes of insanity.] In common language, it is made to signify both a moment and a number of years, consequently it does not comprize any stated time. The term *lucid interval* is therefore relative. As the law requires a precise developement of opinion, I should define a *lucid interval* to be a complete recovery of the patient's intellects, ascertained by repeated examinations of his conversation, and by constant observation of his conduct, for a time sufficient to enable the superintendant to form a correct judgment. Unthinking people, are frequently led to conclude, that if, during a short conversation, a person under confinement shall bewray nothing absurd or incorrect, he is well, and often remonstrate on the injustice of secluding him from the world. Even in common society, there are many persons whom we never suspect, from a few trifling topics of discourse, to be shallow minded; but, if we start a subject, and wish to discuss it through all its ramifications and dependancies, we find them incapable of pursuing a connected chain of reasoning. In the same manner insane people will often, for a short time, conduct themselves, both in conversation and behaviour, with such propriety, that they appear to have the just exercise and direction of their faculties: but let the examiner protract the discourse until the favourite subject shall have got afloat in the mad man's brain, and he will be convinced of the hastiness of his decision. To those unaccustomed to insane people, a few coherent sentences, or rational answers, would indicate a lucid interval, because they discovered no madness; but he, who is in possession of the peculiar turn of the patient's thoughts, might lead him to disclose them, or by a continuance of the conversation, they would spontaneously break forth. A beautiful illustration of this is contained in the Rasselas of Dr. Johnson, where the astronomer is admired as a person of sound intellect and great acquirements by Imlac, who is himself a philosopher, and a man of the world. His intercourse with the astronomer is frequent; and he always finds in his society information and delight. At length he receives Imlac into the most unbounded confidence, and imparts to him the momentous secret. "Hear, Imlac, what thou wilt not, without difficulty, credit. I have possessed, for five years, the regulation of weather, and the distribution of the seasons. The Sun has listened to my dictates, and passed from tropic to tropic by my direction. The clouds, at my call, have poured their waters, and the Nile has overflowed at my command. I have restrained the rage of the Dog-star, and mitigated the fervours of the Crab. The winds alone, of all the elemental powers, have hitherto refused my authority; and multitudes have perished by equinoctial tempests, which I found myself unable to prohibit or restrain. I have administered this great office with exact justice, and made to the different nations of the earth an impartial dividend of rain and sunshine. What must have been the misery of half the globe, if I had limited the clouds to particular regions, or confined the Sun to either side of the Equator?"

A real case came under my observation some years ago, and which is equally apposite to the subject. A young man had become insane from habitual intoxication; and, during the violence of his disorder, had attempted to destroy himself. Under a supposed imputation of having unnatural propensities, he had amputated his penis, with a view of precluding any future insinuations of that nature. For many months, after he was admitted into the hospital, he continued in a state which obliged him to be strictly confined, as he constantly meditated his own destruction. On a sudden, he became apparently well, was highly sensible of the delusion under which he had laboured, and conversed, as any other person, upon the ordinary topics of discourse. There was, however, something in the reserve of his manner, and peculiarity of his look, which persuaded me he was not well, although no incoherence could be detected in his conversation. I had observed him for some days to walk rather lame, and once or twice had noticed him sitting with his shoes off, rubbing his feet. On enquiring into the motives of his doing so, he replied, that his feet were blistered, and wished that some remedy might be applied to remove the vesications. When I requested to look at his feet, he declined it, and prevaricated, saying, that they were only tender and uncomfortable. In a few days afterwards, he assured me they were perfectly well. The next evening I observed him, unperceived, still rubbing his feet, and then peremptorily insisted on examining them. They were quite free from any disorder. He now told me, with some embarrassment, that he wished much for a confidential friend, to whom he might impart a secret of importance; upon assuring him that he might trust me, he said, that the boards on which he walked, (the second story) were heated by subterraneous fires, under the direction of invisible and malicious agents, whose intentions, he was well convinced, were to consume him by degrees.

From these considerations, I am inclined to think, that a *lucid interval* includes all the circumstances, which I have enumerated in my definition of it. If the person, who is to examine the state of the patient's mind, be unacquainted with his peculiar opinions, he may be easily deceived, because, wanting this information, he will have no clue to direct his enquiries, and madmen do not always, nor immediately intrude their incoherent notions: they have sometimes such a high degree of control over their minds, that when they have any particular purpose to carry, they will affect to renounce those opinions, which shall have been judged inconsistent: and it is well known, that they have often dissembled their resentment, until a favourable opportunity has occurred of gratifying their revenge.

Of this restraint, which madmen have sometimes the power of imposing on their opinions, the remark has been so frequent, that those who are more immediately about their persons, have termed it, in their rude phrase, *stifling the disorder*.

Among the numerous instances of this cunning and dissimulation, which I have witnessed in insane persons, the relation of one case will be sufficient to exemplify the subject.

An Essex farmer, about the middle age, had on one occasion so completely masked his disorder, that I was induced to suppose him well, when he was quite otherwise. He had not been at home many hours, before his derangement was discernable by all those, who came to congratulate him on the recovery of his reason. His impetuosity, and mischievous disposition daily increasing, he was sent to a private mad-house; there being, at that time, no vacancy in the hospital. Almost from the moment of his confinement he became tranquil, and orderly, but remonstrated on the injustice of his seclusion.

Having once deceived me, he wished much, that my opinion should be taken respecting the state of his intellects, and assured his friends that he would submit to my determination. I had taken care to be well prepared for this interview, by obtaining an accurate account of the manner in which he had conducted himself. At this examination, he managed himself with admirable address. He spoke of the treatment he had received, from the persons under whose care he was then placed, as most kind and fatherly: he also expressed himself as particularly fortunate in being under my care, and bestowed many handsome compliments on my skill in treating this disorder, and expatiated on my sagacity in perceiving the slightest tinges of insanity. When I wished him to explain certain parts of his conduct, and particularly some extravagant opinions, respecting certain persons and circumstances, he disclaimed all knowledge of such circumstances, and felt himself hurt, that my mind should have been poisoned so much to his prejudice. He displayed equal subtilty on three other occasions when I visited him; although by protracting the conversation, he let fall sufficient to satisfy my mind that he was a mad-man. In a short time he was removed to the hospital, where he expressed great satisfaction in being under my inspection. The private mad-house, which he had formerly so much commended, now became the subject of severe animadversion; he said that he had there been treated with extreme cruelty; that he had been nearly starved, and eaten up by vermin of various descriptions. On enquiring of some convalescent patients, I found (as I had suspected) that I was as much the subject of abuse, when absent, as any of his supposed enemies; although to my face his behaviour was courteous and respectful. More than a month had elapsed, since his admission into the hospital, before he pressed me for my opinion; probably confiding in his address, and hoping to deceive me. At length he appealed to my decision, and urged the correctness of his conduct during confinement as an argument for his liberation. But when I informed him of circumstances he supposed me unacquainted with, and assured him, that he was a proper subject for the asylum where he then inhabited; he suddenly poured forth a torrent of abuse; talked in the most incoherent manner; insisted on the truth of what he had formerly denied; breathed vengeance against his family and friends, and became so outrageous that it was necessary to order him to be strictly confined. He continued in a state of unceasing fury for more than fifteen months.

As the memory, appears to be particularly defective in cases of insanity, it is much to be wished, that we possessed a correct history, and physiological account of this wonderful faculty. Unfortunately, this knowledge is not to be sought for with much prospect of attainment, from books which treat of the human mind and its philosophy; nor is the present work, to be considered as the depository of such information. A deliberate attention, to the precise order in which we acquire information on any subject; a consideration of the effects of its repetition; an investigation of the result (comparing it to a chain) whenever the links are separated, together with a knowledge of the contrivance of abbreviated signs, would perhaps render the matter sufficiently intelligible. But it would be necessary, thoroughly to understand the nature of the thing, of which the sign has been abbreviated: particularly, as the usual mode of education is satisfied with possessing the convenience of the abbreviation, without any inquiry into the nature of the thing, and the cause of the abbreviation of its sign. This faulty mode of instruction, has furnished us with a profusion of names, and left us ignorant of the things they represent.

Ben Johnson has afforded us the shortest, and probably, the best account of memory.

"*Memory* of all the *powers* of the mind, is the most *delicate*, and frail: It is the first of our *faculties* that age invades. Seneca, the Father, the *Rhetorician*, confesseth of himself, he had a miraculous one, not only to receive, but to hold. I myself could in my youth, have repeated all that ever I had made, and so continued till I was past forty: since it is much decayed in me. Yet I can repeat whole books that I have read, and *Poems* of some selected friends, which I have lik'd to charge my memory with. It was wont to be faithful to me, but shaken with *Age* now, and *Sloth* (which weakens the strongest abilities) it may perform somewhat, but cannot promise much. By exercise it is to be made better and serviceable. Whatsoever I pawn'd with it while I was young and a boy, it offers me readily, and without stops: but what I trust to it now, or have done of later years, it lays up more negligently, and sometimes loses; so that I receive mine own (though frequently called for) as if it were new and borrow'd. Nor do I always find presently from it what I do seek; but while I am doing another thing, that I laboured for will come: and what I sought with trouble, will offer itself when I am quiet. Now in some men I have found it as happy as nature, who, whatsoever they read or pen, they can say without book presently; as if they did then write in their mind. And it is more a wonder in such as have a swift stile, for their Memories are commonly slowest; such as torture their writings, and go into council for every word, must needs fix somewhat, and make it their own at last, though but through their own vexation."—*Discoveries, vol.* vi. *p.* 240, 1716.

If in a chain of ideas, a number of the links are broken, or leaving out the metaphor, if there be an inability to recollect circumstances in the order, in which they occurred, the mind cannot possess any accurate information. When patients of this description are asked a question, they appear as if awakened from a sound sleep: they are searching, they know not where, for the proper materials of an answer, and, in the painful, and fruitless efforts of recollection, generally lose sight of the question itself. Shakespeare, the highest authority in every thing relating to the human mind and its affections, seems to be persuaded, that some defect of memory is necessary to constitute madness.

"It is not madnesse
That I have uttered: bring me to the test
And I the matter will *re-word*, which madnesse
Would gambol from."—*Hamlet, Act* III. *Scene* 4.

In persons of sound mind, as well as in maniacs, the memory is the first power which decays; and there is something remarkable in the manner of its decline. The transactions of the latter part of life are feebly recollected, whilst the scenes of youth and of manhood, remain more strongly impressed.

When I have listened to the conversations of the old incurable patients, the topic has generally turned upon the transactions of early days; and, on the circumstances of that period of life, they have frequently spoken with tolerable correctness. In many cases, where the mind has been injured by intemperance, the same withering of the recollection may be observed. It may, perhaps, arise from the mind at an early period of life, being most susceptible and retentive of impressions, and from a greater disposition to be pleased, with the objects which are presented: whereas, the cold caution, and fastidiousness with which age surveys the prospects of life, joined to the dulness of the senses, and the slight curiosity which prevails, will, in some degree, explain the difficulty of recalling the history of later transactions.

Insane people, who have been good scholars, after a long confinement, lose, in a wonderful degree, the correctness of orthography: when they write, above half the words are frequently mis-spelt, they are written according to the pronunciation. It shews how treacherous the memory is without reinforcement. The same necessity of a constant recruit, and frequent review of our ideas, satisfactorily explains, why a number of patients lapse nearly into a state of ideotism. These have, for some years, been the silent and gloomy inhabitants of the hospital, who have avoided conversation, and courted solitude; consequently have acquired no new ideas, and time has effaced the impression of those, formerly stamped on the mind. Mr. Locke, well observes, although he speaks figuratively, "that there seems to be a constant decay of all our ideas, even of those which are struck deepest, and in minds the most retentive; so that, if they be not sometimes renewed by repeated exercise of the senses, or reflection on those kind of objects, which at first occasioned them, the print wears out, and at last there remains nothing to be seen."

Connected with loss of memory, there is a form of insanity which occurs in young persons; and, as far as these cases have been the subject of my observation, they have been more frequently noticed in females. Those whom I have seen, have been distinguished by prompt capacity and lively disposition: and in general have become the favourites of parents and tutors, by their facility in acquiring knowledge, and by a prematurity of attainment. This disorder commences, about, or shortly after, the period of menstruation, and in many instances has been unconnected with hereditary taint; as far as could be ascertained by minute enquiry. The attack is almost imperceptible; some months usually elapse, before it becomes the subject of particular notice; and fond relatives are frequently deceived by the hope that it is only an abatement of excessive vivacity, conducing to a prudent reserve, and steadiness of character. A degree of apparent thoughtfulness and inactivity precede, together with a diminution of the ordinary curiosity, concerning that which is passing before them; and they therefore neglect those objects and pursuits which formerly proved sources of delight and instruction. The sensibility appears to be considerably blunted; they do not bear the same affection towards their parents and relations; they become unfeeling to kindness, and careless of reproof. To their companions they shew a cold civility, but take no interest whatever in their concerns. If they read a book, they are unable to give any account of its contents: sometimes, with steadfast eyes, they will dwell for an hour on one page, and then turn over a number in a few minutes. It is very difficult to persuade them to write, which most readily develops their state of mind: much time is consumed and little produced. The subject is repeatedly begun, but they seldom advance beyond a sentence or two: the orthography becomes puzzling, and by endeavouring to adjust the spelling, the subject vanishes. As their apathy increases they are negligent of their dress, and inattentive to personal cleanliness. Frequently they seem to experience transient impulses of passion, but these have no source in sentiment; the tears, which trickle down at one time, are as unmeaning as the loud laugh which succeeds them; and it often happens that a momentary gust of anger, with its attendant invectives, ceases before the threat can be concluded. As the disorder increases, the urine and fæces are passed without restraint, and from the indolence which accompanies it, they generally become corpulent. Thus in the interval between puberty and manhood, I have painfully witnessed this hopeless and degrading change, which in a short time has transformed the most promising and vigorous intellect into a slavering and bloated ideot.

Of the organs of sense, which become affected in those labouring under insanity, the ear, more particularly suffers. I scarcely recollect an instance of a lunatic becoming blind, but numbers are deaf. It is also certain that in these persons, more delusion is conveyed through the ear than the eye, or any of the other senses. Those who are not actually deaf, are troubled with difficulty of hearing, and tinnitus aurium. Thus an insane person shall suppose that he has received a commission from the Deity; that he has ordered him to make known his word, or to perform some act, as a manifestation of his will and power. It is however much to be regretted, that these divine commissions generally terminate in human mischief and calamity, and instances are not unfrequent, where these holy inspirations, have urged the unfortunate believer to strangle his wife, and attempt the butchery of his children. From this source may be explained, the numerous delusions of modern prophecies, which circumstantially relate the gossipings of angels, and record the hallucinations of feverish repose.

In consequence of some affection of the ear, the insane sometimes insist that malicious agents contrive to blow streams of infected air into this organ: others have conceived, by means of what they term hearkening wires and whiz-pipes, that various obscenities and blasphemies are forced into their minds; and it is not unusual for those who are in a desponding condition, to assert, that they distinctly hear the devil tempting them to self-destruction.

A considerable portion of the time of many lunatics, is passed in replies to something supposed to be uttered. As this is an increasing habit, so it may be considered as an unfavourable symptom, and at last the patient becomes so abstracted from surrounding objects, that the greater part of the day is consumed in giving answers to these supposed communications. It sometimes happens that the intelligence conveyed, is of a nature to provoke the mad-man, and on these occasions, he generally exercises his wrath on the nearest bystander; whom he supposes, in the hurry of his anger, to be the offending party.

In the soundest state of our faculties, we are more liable to be deceived by the ear, than through the medium of the other senses: a partial obstruction by wax, shall cause the person so affected, to hear the bubbling of water, the ringing of bells, or the sounds of musical instruments; and on some occasions, although the relation seems tinged with superstition, men of undeviating veracity, and of the highest attainments, have asserted, that they have heard themselves *called*. "He [Dr. Johnson] mentioned a thing as not unfrequent, of which I [Mr. Boswell] had never heard before—being *called*, that is, hearing one's name pronounced by the voice of a known person at a great distance, far beyond the possibility of being reached by any sound, uttered by human organs. An acquaintance on whose veracity I can depend, told me, that walking home one evening to Kilmarnock, he heard himself called from a wood, by the voice of a brother who had gone to America; and the next packet brought account of that brother's death. Macbean asserted that this inexplicable *calling* was a thing very well known. Dr. Johnson said, that one day at Oxford, as he was turning the key of his chamber, he heard his mother distinctly call *Sam*. She was then at Litchfield; but nothing ensued. This phænomenon is, I think, as wonderful as any other mysterious fact, which many people are very slow to believe, or rather, indeed, reject with an obstinate contempt."— *Boswell's Life of Dr. Johnson*, 4to. vol. ii. p. 384.

One of the most curious cases of this nature which has fallen under my observation, I shall here venture to relate, for the amusement of the reader. The patient was a well educated man, about the middle age; he always stopped his ears closely with wool, and, in addition to a flannel night-cap, usually slept with his head in a tin saucepan. Being asked the reason why he so fortified his head, he replied, "To prevent the intrusion of the *sprites*." After having made particular enquiry concerning the nature of these beings, he gravely communicated the following information:—"Sir, you must know that in the human seminal fluid there are a number of vital particles, which being injected into the female, impregnate her, and form a fœtus of muscles and bones. But this fluid has other properties, it is capable, by itself, of producing vitality under certain circumstances, and experienced chemists and hermetical philosophers have devised a method of employing it for other purposes, and some, the most detrimental to the condition and happiness of man. These philosophers, who are in league with princes, and their convenient and prostituted agents, contrive to extract a portion of their own semen, which they conserve in rum or brandy: these liquors having the power of holding for a considerable time the seminal fluid, and keeping its vitality uninjured. When these secret agents intend to perform any of their devilish experiments on a person, who is an object of suspicion to any of these potentates, they cunningly introduce themselves to his acquaintance, lull him to sleep by artificial means, and during his slumbers, infuse a portion of their seminal fluid (conserved in rum or brandy) into his ears.

"As the semen in the natural commerce with the woman, produces a child, so, having its vitality conserved by the spirit, it becomes capable of forming a *sprite*; a term, obviously derived from the spirit in which it had been infused. The ear is the most convenient nidus for hatching these vital particles of the semen. The effects produced on the individual, during the incubation of these seminal germs, are very disagreeable; they cause the blood to mount into the head, and produce considerable giddiness and confusion of thought. In a short time, they acquire the size of a pin's head; and then they perforate the drum of the ear, which enables them to traverse the interior of the brain, and become acquainted with the hidden secrets of the person's mind. During the time they are thus educated, they enlarge according to the natural laws of growth; they then take wing, and become invisible beings, and, from the strong ties of natural affection, assisted by the principle of attraction, they revert to the parent who afforded the semen, and communicate to him their surreptitious observations and intellectual gleanings. In this manner, I have been defrauded of discoveries which would have entitled me to opulence and distinction, and have lived to see others reap honours and emoluments, for speculations which were the genuine offsprings of my own brain."

By some persons, madness has been considered as a state of mind analogous to dreaming: but an inference of this kind supposes us fully acquainted with the actual state, or condition of the mind in dreaming, and in madness. The whole question hinges on a knowledge of this *state of mind*, which I fear is still involved in obscurity. As it is not the object of the present work to discuss this curious question, the reader is referred to the fifth section of the first part of Mr. Dugald Stewart's Elements of the Philosophy of the Human Mind, and to the note, o, at the end; he will also find the subject treated with considerable ingenuity in the eleventh section of Mr. Brown's Observations on Zoonomia.

There is, however, a circumstance, which to my knowledge, has not been noticed by those who have treated on this subject, and which appears to establish a marked distinction between madness and dreaming. In madness, the delusion we experience is most frequently conveyed through the ear; in dreaming, the deception is commonly optical; we see much, and hear little; indeed dreaming, at least with myself, seems to be a species of intelligible pantomime, that does not require the aid of language to explain it. It is true, that some who have perfectly recovered from this disease, and who are persons of good understanding and liberal education, describe the state they were in, as resembling a dream: and when they have been told how long they were disordered, have been astonished that the time passed so rapidly away. But this only refers to that consciousness of delusion, which is admitted by the patient on his return to reason; in the same manner as the man awake, smiles at the incongruous images, and abrupt transitions of the preceding night. In neither condition, does the consciousness of delusion, establish any thing explanatory of the *state* of the mind.

In a description of madness, it would be blameable to omit a form of this disease which is commonly very intractable, and of the most alarming consequences; I mean, the insanity which arises from the habit of intoxication. All persons who have had any experience of this disease, readily allow that fermented liquors, taken to excess, are capable of producing mental derangement: but the medical practitioner has in such cases, to contend, and generally without effect, with popular prejudice, and sometimes, with the subordinate advisers of the law.

To constitute madness, the minds of ignorant people expect a display of continued violence, and they are not satisfied that the person can be pronounced in that state, without they see him exhibit the pranks of a baboon, or hear him roar and bellow like a beast. By these people the patient is stated only to be intemperate; they confess that he does very foolish things when intoxicated; but that he is not mad, and only requires to be restrained from drinking. Thus, a man is permitted slowly to poison and destroy himself; to produce a state of irritation, which disqualifies him for any of the useful purposes of life; to squander his property amongst the most worthless and abandoned; to communicate a loathsome and disgraceful disease to a virtuous wife, and leave an innocent and helpless family to the meager protection of the parish. If it be possible, the law ought to define the circumstances, under which it becomes justifiable, to restrain a human being from effecting his own destruction, and involving his family in misery and ruin. When a man suddenly bursts through the barriers of established opinions; if he attempt to strangle himself with a cord, to divide his larger blood-vessels with a knife, or swallow a vial full of laudanum, no one entertains any doubt of his being a proper subject for the superintendance of keepers, but he is allowed, without control, by a gradual process, to undermine the fabric of his own health, and destroy the prosperity of his family.

All patients have not the same degree of memory of what has passed during the time they were disordered: and I have frequently remarked, when they were unable to give any account of the peculiar opinions which they had indulged, during a raving paroxysm of long continuance, that they well remembered any coercion which had been used, or any kindness which had been shewn them.

Insane people, are said to be generally worse in the morning; in some cases they certainly are so, but perhaps not so frequently as has been supposed. In many instances (and, as far as I have observed) in the beginning of the disease, they are more violent in the evening, and continue so the greatest part of the night. It is, however, a certain fact, that the majority of patients of this description, have their symptoms aggravated by being placed in a recumbent posture. They seem, themselves, to avoid the horizontal position as much as possible, when they are in a raving state: and when so confined that they cannot be erect, will keep themselves seated upon the breech.

Many of those who are violently disordered will continue particular actions for a considerable time: some are heard to gingle the chain, with which they are confined, for hours without intermission; others, who are secured in an erect posture, will beat the ground with their feet the greatest part of the day. Upon enquiry of such patients, after they have recovered, they have assured me that these actions afforded them considerable relief. We often surprize persons who are supposed free from any mental derangement, in many strange and ridiculous movements, particularly if their minds be intently occupied:[7]—this does not appear to be so much the effect of habit, as of a particular state of mind.

Among the bodily particularities which mark this disease, may be observed the protruded, and oftentimes glistening eye, and a peculiar cast of countenance, which, however, cannot be described. In some, an appearance takes place which has not hitherto been noticed by authors. This is a relaxation of the integuments of the cranium, by which they may be wrinkled, or rather gathered up by the hand to a considerable degree. It is generally most remarkable on the posterior part of the scalp; as far as my enquiries have reached, it does not take place in the beginning of the disease, but after a raving paroxysm of some continuance. It has been frequently accompanied with contraction of the iris.

On the suggestion of a medical gentleman, I was induced to ascertain the prevailing complexion and colour of the hair in insane patients. Out of two hundred and sixty-five who were examined, two hundred and five were of a swarthy complexion, with dark, or black hair; the remaining sixty were of a fair skin, and light, brown, or redhaired. What connexion this proportion may have, with the complexion and colour of the hair of the people of this country in general, and what alterations may have been produced by age, or a residence in other climates, I am totally uninformed.

Of the power which maniacs possess of resisting cold, the belief is general, and the histories which are on record are truly wonderful: it is not my wish to disbelieve, nor my intention to dispute them; it is proper, however, to state that the patients in Bethlem Hospital possess no such exemption from the effects of severe cold. They are particularly subject to mortifications of the feet; and this fact is so well established from former accidents, that there is an express order of the house, that every patient, under strict confinement, shall have his feet examined morning and evening in the cold weather by the keeper, and also have them constantly wrapped in flannel; and those who are permitted to go about, are always to be found as near to the fire as they can get, during the winter season.

From the great degree of insensibility which prevails in some states of madness, a degree of cold would scarcely be felt by such persons, which would create uneasiness in those of sound mind; but experience has shewn that they suffer equally from severity of weather. When the mind is particularly engaged on any subject, external circumstances affect us less than when unoccupied. Every one must recollect that, in following up a favourite pursuit, his fire has burned out, without his being sensible of the alteration of temperature; but when the performance has been finished, or he has become indifferent to it from fatigue, he then becomes sensible to cold, which he had not experienced before.

Some maniacs refuse all covering, but these are not common occurrences; and it may be presumed, that by a continued exposure to the atmosphere, such persons might sustain, with impunity, a low temperature, which would be productive of serious injury to those who are clad according to the exigences of the season. Such endurance of cold is more probably the effect of habit, than of any condition peculiar to insanity.

Having thus given a general account of the symptoms, I shall now lay before my readers a history of the appearances which I have noticed on opening the heads of several maniacs who have died in Bethlem Hospital.

CHAP. III.

CASES, WITH THE APPEARANCES ON DISSECTION.

CASE I.

J. H. a man twenty-eight years of age, was admitted a patient in May, 1795. He had been disordered for about two months before he came into the hospital. No particular cause was stated to have brought on the complaint. It was most probably an hereditary affection, as his father had been several times insane and confined in our hospital. During the time he was in the house, he was in a very low and melancholic state; shewed an aversion to food, and said he was resolved to die. His obstinacy in refusing all nourishment was very great, and it was with much difficulty forced upon him. He continued in this state, but became daily weaker and more emaciated until August 1st, when he died. Upon opening the head, the pericranium was found loosely adherent to the scull. The bones of the cranium were thick. The pia mater was loaded with blood, and the medullary substance, when cut into, was full of bloody points. The pineal gland contained a large quantity of gritty matter.[8] The consistence of the brain was natural; he was opened twenty-four hours after death.

CASE II.

J. W. was a man of sixty-two years of age, who had been many years in the house as an incurable patient, but with the other parts of whose history I am totally unacquainted. He appeared to be a quiet and inoffensive person, who found amusement in his own thoughts, and seldom joined in any conversation with the other patients: for some months he had been troubled with a cough, attended with copious expectoration, which very much reduced him; dropsical symptoms followed these complaints. He became every day weaker, and on July 10th, 1795, died. He was opened eighteen hours after death. The pericranium adhered loosely to the scull; the bones of the cranium were unusually thin. There were slight opacities in many parts of the tunica arachnoidea; in the ventricles about four ounces of water were contained—some large hydatids were discovered on the plexus choroides of the right side. The consistence of the brain was natural.

CASE III.

G. H. a man twenty-six years of age, was received into the hospital, July 18th, 1795. It was stated that he had been disordered six weeks previously to his admission, and that he never had any former attack. He had been a drummer with a recruiting party, and had been for some time in the habit of constant intoxication, which was assigned as the cause of his insanity. He continued in a violent and raving state about a month, during the whole of which time he got little or no sleep. He had no knowledge of his situation, but supposed himself with the regiment, and was frequently under great anxiety and alarm for the loss of his drum, which he imagined had been stolen and sold. The medicines which were given to him he conceived were spirituous liquors, and swallowed them with avidity. At the expiration of a month he was very weak and reduced; his legs became œdematous— his pupils were much diminished. He now believed himself a child, called upon the people about him as his playfellows, and appeared to recal the scenes of early life with facility and correctness. Within a few days of his decease he only muttered to himself. August 26th, he died. He was opened six hours after death. The pericranium was loosely adherent. The tunica arachnoidea had generally lost its transparency, and was considerably thickened. The veins of the pia mater were loaded with blood, and in many places seemed to contain air. There was a considerable quantity of water between the membranes, and, as nearly as could be ascertained, about four ounces in the ventricles, in the cavity of which, the veins appeared remarkably turgid. The consistence of the brain was more than usually firm.

CASE IV.

E. M. a woman, aged sixty, was admitted into the house, August 8th, 1795; she had been disordered five months: the cause assigned was extreme grief, in consequence of the loss of her only daughter. She was very miserable and restless; conceived she had been accused of some horrid crime, for which she apprehended she should be burned alive. When any persons entered her room she supposed them officers of justice, who were about to drag her to some cruel punishment. She was frequently violent, and would strike and bite those who came near her. Upon the idea that she should shortly be put to death, she refused all sustenance; and it became necessary to force her to take it. In this state she continued, growing daily weaker and more emaciated, until October 3d, when she died.

Upon opening the head, there was a copious determination of blood to the whole contents of the cranium. The pia mater was considerably inflamed; there was not any water either in the ventricles or between the membranes. The brain was particularly soft. She was opened thirty hours after death.

CASE V.

W. P. a young man, aged twenty-five, was admitted into the hospital, September 26th, 1795. He had been disordered five months, and had experienced a similar attack six years before. The disease was brought on by excessive drinking. He was in a very furious state, in consequence of which he was constantly confined. He very seldom slept—during the greater part of the night he was singing, or swearing, or holding conversations with persons he imagined to be about him: sometimes he would rattle the chain with which he was confined, for several hours together, and tore every thing to pieces within his reach. In the beginning of November, the violence of his disorder subsided for two or three days, but afterwards returned; and on the 10th he died compleatly exhausted by his exertions.—Upon opening the head the pericranium was found firmly attached; the pia mater was inflamed, though not to any very considerable degree; the tunica arachnoidea in some places was slightly shot with blood; the membranes of the brain, and its convolutions, when these were removed, were of a brown, or brownish straw colour. There was no water in any of the cavities of the brain, nor any particular congestion of blood in its substance—the consistence of which was natural. He was opened twenty hours after death.

CASE VI.

B. H. was an incurable patient, who had been confined in the house from the year 1788, and for some years before that time in a private madhouse. He was about sixty years of age—had formerly been in the habit of intoxicating himself. His character was strongly marked by pride, irascibility, and malevolence. During the four last years of his life, he was confined for attempting to commit some violence on one of the officers of the house. After this, he was seldom heard to speak; yet he manifested his evil disposition by every species of dumb insult. Latterly he grew suspicious, and would sometimes tell the keeper that his victuals were poisoned. About the beginning of December he was taken ill with a cough, attended with copious expectoration. Being then asked respecting his complaints, he said, he had a violent pain across the stomach, which arose from his navel string at his birth having been tied too short. He never spoke afterwards, though frequently importuned to describe his complaints. He died December 24, 1795.

Upon dividing the integuments of the head, the pericranium was found scarcely to adhere to the scull. On the right parietal bone there was a large blotch, as if the bone had been inflamed: there were others on different parts of the bone, but considerably smaller. The glandulæ Pacchioni were uncommonly large: the tunica arachnoidea in many places wanted the natural transparency of that membrane: there was a large determination of blood to the substance of the brain: the ventricles contained about three ounces of water: the consistence of the brain was natural. He was opened two days after death.

CASE VII.

A. M. a woman, aged twenty-seven, was admitted into the hospital, August 15, 1795; she had then been eleven weeks disordered. Religious enthusiasm, and a too frequent attendance on conventicles, were stated to have occasioned her complaint. She was in a very miserable and unhappy condition, and terrified by the most alarming apprehensions for the salvation of her soul. Towards the latter end of September, she appeared in a convalescent state, and continued tolerably well until the middle of November, when she began to relapse.

The return of her disorder commenced with loss of sleep. She alternately sang, and cried the greatest part of the night. She conceived her inside full of the most loathsome vermin, and often felt the sensation as if they were crawling into her throat. She was suddenly seized with a strong and unconquerable determination to destroy herself; became very sensible of her malady, and said, that God had inflicted this punishment on her, from having (at some former part of her life) said the Lord's Prayer backwards. She continued some time in a restless and forlorn state; at one moment expecting the devil to seize upon her and tear her to pieces; in the next, wondering that she was not instigated to commit violence on the persons about her. On January 12, 1796, she died suddenly. She was opened twelve hours after death. The thoracic and abdominal viscera were perfectly healthy.

Upon examining the contents of the cranium, the pia mater was considerably inflamed, and an extravasated blotch, about the size of a shilling, was seen upon that membrane, near the middle of the right lobe of the cerebrum. There was no water between the membranes, nor in the ventricles, but a general determination of blood to the contents of the cranium. The medullary substance, when cut into, was full of bloody points. The consistence of the brain was natural.

CASE VIII.

M. W. a very tall and thin woman, forty-four years of age, was admitted into the hospital, September 19, 1795. Her disorder was of six months standing, and eight years before she had also had an attack of this disease. The cause assigned to have brought it on, the last time, was the loss of some property, the disease having shortly followed that circumstance.—The constant tenor of her discourse was, that she should live but a short time. She seemed anxiously to wish for her dissolution, but had no thoughts of accomplishing her own destruction. In the course of a few weeks she began to imagine, that some malevolent person had given her mercury with an intention to destroy her. She was constantly shewing her teeth, which had decayed naturally, as if this effect had been produced by that medicine: at last she insisted, that mercurial preparations were mingled in the food and medicines which were administered to her. Her appetite was voracious, notwithstanding this belief. She had a continual thirst, and drank very large quantities of cold water.

On January 14, 1796, she had an apoplectic fit, well marked by stertor, loss of voluntary motion, and insensibility to stimuli. On the following day she died. She was opened two days after death. There was a remarkable accumulation of blood in the veins of the dura and pia mater; the substance of the brain was loaded with blood. When the medullary substance was cut into, blood oozed from it; and, upon squeezing it, a greater quantity could be forced out. On the pia mater covering the right lobe of the cerebrum, were some slight extravasations of blood. The ventricles contained no water; on the plexus choroides were some vesicles of the size of coriander-seeds, filled with a yellow fluid. The pericranium adhered firmly to the scull. The consistence of the brain was firmer than usual.

CASE IX.

E. D. a woman, aged thirty-six, was admitted into the hospital, February 20, 1795; she had then been disordered four months. Her insanity came on a few days after having been delivered. She had also laboured under a similar attack seven years before, which, like the present, supervened upon the birth of a child. Under the impression that she ought to be hanged, she destroyed her infant, with the view of meeting with that punishment. When she came into the house, she was very sensible of the crime she had committed, and felt the most poignant affliction for the act. For about a month she continued to amend: after which time she became more thoughtful, and frequently spoke about the child: great anxiety and restlessness succeeded. In this state she remained until April 23, when her tongue became thickly furred, the skin parched, her eyes inflamed and glassy, and her pulse quick. She now talked incoherently; and, towards the evening, merely muttered to herself. She died on the following day comatose.

She was opened about twenty-four hours after death. The scull was thick, the pericranium scarcely adhered to the bone, the dura mater was also but slightly attached to its internal surface. There was a large quantity of water between the dura mater and tunica arachnoidea; this latter membrane was much thickened, and was of a milky white appearance. Between the tunica arachnoidea and pia mater, there was a considerable accumulation of water. The veins of the pia mater were particularly turgid. About three ounces of water were contained in the lateral ventricles: the veins of the membrane lining these cavities were remarkably large and turgid with blood. When the medullary substance of the cerebrum and cerebellum was cut into, there appeared a great number of bloody points. The brain was of its natural consistence.

CASE X.

C. M. a man, forty years of age, was admitted into the hospital, December 26, 1795. It was stated, that he had been disordered two months previously to his having been received as a patient. His friends were unacquainted with any cause, which was likely to have induced the disease. During the time he was in the house he seemed sulky, or rather stupid. He never asked any questions, and if spoken to, either replied shortly, or turned away without giving any answer. He scarcely appeared to take notice of any thing which was going forward, and if told to do any little office generally forgot what he was going about, before he had advanced half a dozen steps. He remained in this state until the beginning of May, 1796, when his legs became œdematous, and his abdomen swollen. He grew very feeble and helpless, and died rather suddenly, May 19th. He was opened about forty-eight hours after death. The pericranium and dura mater adhered firmly to the scull; in many places there was an opake whiteness of the tunica arachnoidea. About four ounces of water were found in the ventricles. The plexus choroides were uncommonly pale. The medullary substance afforded hardly any bloody points when cut into. The consistence of the brain I cannot describe better than by saying, it was doughy.

CASE XI.

S. M. a man, thirty-six years of age, was admitted as an incurable patient in the year 1790. Of the former history of his complaint I have no information. As his habits, which frequently came under my observation, were of a singular nature, it may not here be improper to relate them.—Having at some period of his confinement been mischievously disposed, and, in consequence, put under coercion, he never afterwards found himself comfortable when at liberty. When he rose in the morning he went immediately to the room where he was usually confined, and placed himself in a particular corner, until the keeper came to secure him. If he found any other patient had pre-occupied his situation, he became very outrageous, and generally forced them to leave it. When he had been confined, for which he appeared anxious, as he bore any delay with little temper, he employed himself throughout the remainder of the day, by tramping or shuffling his feet. He was constantly muttering to himself, of which scarcely one word in a sentence was intelligible. When an audible expression escaped him it was commonly an imprecation. If a stranger visited him, he always asked for tobacco, but seldom repeated his solicitation. He devoured his food with avidity, and always muttered as he ate.

In the month of July, 1796, he was seized with a diarrhœa, which afterwards terminated in dysentery. This continued, notwithstanding the employment of every medicine usually given in such a case, until his death, which took place on September 23, of the same year. He was opened twelve hours after death. The scull was unusually thin; the glandulæ Pacchioni were large and numerous: there was a very general determination of blood to the brain: the medullary substance, when cut, shewed an abundance of bloody points: the lateral ventricles contained about four ounces of water: the consistence of the brain was natural.

CASE XII.

E. R. was a woman, to all appearance about eighty years of age, but of whose history, before she came into the hospital, it has not been in my power to acquire any satisfactory intelligence. She was an incurable patient, and had been admitted on that establishment in February, 1782.

During the time I had an opportunity of observing her, she continued in the same state: she appeared feeble and childish. During the course of the day, she sat in a particular part of the common-room, from which she never stirred. Her appetite was tolerably good, but it was requisite to feed her. Except she was particularly urged to speak she never talked. As the summer declined she grew weaker, and died October 19, 1796, apparently worn out. She was opened two days after death. The scull was particularly thin; the pericranium adhered firmly to the bone, and the scull-cap was with difficulty separated from the dura mater. There was a very large quantity of water between the membranes of the brain: the glandulæ Pacchioni were uncommonly large: the tunica arachnoidea was in many places blotched and streaked with opacities: when the medullary substance of the brain was cut into, it was every where bloody; and blood could be pressed from it, as from a sponge. There were some large hydatids on the plexus choroides: in the ventricles about a tea spoonful of water was observed: the consistence of the brain was particularly firm, but it could not be called elastic. There were no symptoms of general dropsy.

CASE XIII.

J. D. a man, thirty-five years of age, was admitted into the hospital in October, 1796. He was a person of good education, and had been regularly brought up to medicine, which he had practised in this town for several years. It was stated by his friends, that, about two years before, he had suffered a similar attack, which continued six months: but it appears from the observations of some medical persons, that he never perfectly recovered from it, although he returned to the exercise of his profession. A laborious attention to business, and great apprehensions of the want of success, were assigned as causes of his malady. In the beginning of the year 1796 the disease recurred, and became so violent that it was necessary to confine him.

At the time he was received into Bethlem hospital, he was in an unquiet state, got little or no sleep, and was constantly speaking loudly: in general he was worse towards evening. He appeared little sensible of external objects: his exclamations were of the most incoherent nature.

During the time he was a patient he was thrice cupped on the scalp. After each operation, he became rational to a certain degree; but these intervals were of a short continuance, as he relapsed in the course of a few hours. The scalp, particularly at the posterior part of the head, was so loose that a considerable quantity of it could be gathered up by the hand.[9] The violence of his exertions at last exhausted him, and on December 11, he died. He was opened about twenty-four hours after death. There was a large quantity of water between the dura mater and tunica arachnoidea, and also between this latter membrane and the pia mater. The tunica arachnoidea was thickened and opake; the vessels of the pia mater were loaded with blood: when the medullary substance was cut into, it was very abundant in bloody points: about three ounces of water were contained in the lateral ventricles: the plexus choroides were remarkably turgid with blood: a quantity of water was found in the theca vertebralis: the consistence of the brain was natural.

CASE XIV.

J. C. a man, aged sixty-one, was admitted into the hospital September 17, 1796. It was stated, that he had been disordered ten months. He had for thirty years kept a public house, and had for some time been in the habit of getting intoxicated. His memory was considerably impaired: circumstances were so feebly impressed on his mind, that he was unable to give any account of the preceding day. He appeared perfectly reconciled to his situation, and conducted himself with order and propriety. As he seldom spoke but when interrogated, it was not possible to collect his opinions. In this quiet state he continued about two months, when he became more thoughtful and abstracted, walked about with a quick step, and frequently started, as if suddenly interrupted. He was next seized with trembling, appeared anxious to be released from his confinement: conceived at one time that his house was filled with company; at another that different people had gone off without paying him, and that he should be arrested for sums of money which he owed. Under this constant alarm and disquietude he continued about a week, when he became sullen, and refused his food. When importuned to take nourishment, he said it was ridiculous to offer it to him, as he had no mouth to eat it: though forced to take it, he continued in the same opinion; and when food was put into his mouth, insisted that a wound had been made in his throat, in order to force it into his stomach. The next day he complained of violent pain in his head, and in a few minutes afterwards died. He was opened twelve hours after death. There was a large quantity of water between the tunica arachnoidea and pia mater; the latter membrane was much suffused with blood, and many of its vessels were considerably enlarged: the lateral ventricles contained at least six ounces of water: the brain was very firm.

CASE XV.

J. A. a man, forty-two years of age, was first admitted into the house on June 27, 1795. His disease came on suddenly whilst he was working in a garden, on a very hot day, without any covering to his head. He had some years before travelled with a gentleman over a great part of Europe: his ideas ran particularly on what he had seen abroad; sometimes he conceived himself the king of Denmark, at other times the king of France. Although naturally dull and wanting common education, he professed himself a master of all the dead and living languages; but his most intimate acquaintance was with the old French: and he was persuaded he had some faint recollection of coming over to this country with William the Conqueror. His temper was very irritable, and he was disposed to quarrel with every body about him. After he had continued ten months in the hospital, he became tranquil, relinquished his absurdities, and was discharged well in June 1796. He went into the country with his wife to settle some domestic affairs, and in about six weeks afterwards relapsed. He was re-admitted into the hospital August 13th.

He now evidently had a paralytic affection; his speech was inarticulate, and his mouth drawn aside. He shortly became stupid, his legs swelled, and afterwards ulcerated: at length his appetite failed him; he became emaciated, and died December 27th, of the same year. The head was opened twenty hours after death. There was a greater quantity of water between the different membranes of the brain than has ever occurred to me. The tunica arachnoidea was generally opake and very much thickened: the pia mater was loaded with blood, and the veins of that membrane were particularly enlarged. On the forepart of the right hemisphere of the brain, when stripped of its membranes, there was a blotch, of a brown colour, several shades darker than the rest of the cortical substance: the ventricles were much enlarged, and contained, by estimation, at least six ounces of water. The veins in these cavities were particularly turgid. The consistence of the brain was firmer than usual.

CASE XVI.

J. H. a man, aged forty-two, was admitted into the house on April 12, 1794. He had then been disordered two months: it was a family disease on his father's side. Having manifested a mischievous disposition to some of his relations, he was continued in the hospital upon the incurable establishment. His temper was naturally violent, and he was easily provoked. As long as he was kept to any employment he conducted himself tolerably well; but when unoccupied, would walk about in a hurried and distracted manner, throwing out the most horrid threats and imprecations. He would often appear to be holding conversations: but these conferences always terminated in a violent quarrel between the imaginary being and himself. He constantly supposed unfriendly people were placed in different parts of the house to torment and annoy him. However violently he might be contesting any subject with these supposed enemies, if directed by the keepers to render them any assistance, he immediately gave up the dispute and went with alacrity. As he slept but little, the greatest part of the night was spent in a very noisy and riotous manner. In this state he continued until April 1796, when he was attacked with a paralytic affection, which deprived him of the use of the left side. His articulation was now hardly intelligible; he became childish, got gradually weaker, and died December 28, 1796. He was opened twenty-four hours after death. There was a general opacity of the tunica arachnoidea, and a small quantity of water between that membrane and the pia mater: the ventricles were much enlarged and contained a considerable quantity of water, by estimation, four ounces; the consistence of the brain was natural.

CASE XVII.

M. G. a woman, about fifty years of age, had been admitted on the incurable establishment in July 1785. She had for some years before been in a disordered state, and was considered as a dangerous patient. Her temper was violent; and if interrupted in her usual habits, she became very furious. Like many others among the incurables, she was an insulated being: she never spoke except when disturbed. Her greatest delight appeared to be in getting into some corner to sleep; and the interval between breakfast and dinner, was usually past in this manner. At other times she was generally committing some petty mischief, such as slyly breaking a window, dirtying the rooms of the other patients, or purloining their provisions. She had been for some months in a weak and declining state, but would never give any account of her disorder. On January 5, 1797, she died, apparently worn out. The head was opened three days after death. The pericranium adhered but slightly to the scull, nor was the dura mater firmly attached. There was water between the membranes of the brain; and the want of transparency of the tunica arachnoidea, indicated marks of former inflammation. The posterior part of the hemispheres of the brain was of a brownish colour. In this case there was a considerable appearance of air in the veins; the medullary substance, when cut, was full of bloody points: the lateral ventricles were small, but filled with water: the plexus choroides were loaded with vesicles of a much larger size than usual: the consistence of the brain was natural.

CASE XVIII.

S. T. a woman, aged fifty-seven, was admitted into the house, January 14, 1797. It was stated by her friends, that she had been disordered eight months: they were unacquainted with any cause, which might have induced the disease. She had evidently suffered a paralytic attack, which considerably affected her speech, and occasioned her to walk lame with the right leg. As she avoided all conversation, it was not possible to collect any further account of her case. Three days after her admission, she had another paralytic stroke, which deprived her entirely of the use of the right side. Two days afterwards she died. She was opened forty-eight hours after death. There was a small quantity of water between the tunica arachnoidea and pia mater, and a number of opake spots on the former membrane. On the pia mater, covering the posterior part of the left hemisphere of the brain, there was an extravasated blotch, about the size of a shilling: the medullary substance was unusually loaded with blood: the lateral ventricles were large, but did not contain much water: the consistence of the brain was very soft.

CASE XIX.

W. C. a man, aged sixty-three, was admitted into the hospital, January 21, 1797. The persons, who attended at his admission, deposed, that he had been disordered five months; that he never had been insane before, and that the disease came on shortly after the death of his son. He was in a very anxious and miserable state. No persuasion could induce him to take nourishment; and it was with extreme difficulty that any food could be forced upon him. He paced about with an hurried step; was often suddenly struck with the idea of having important business to adjust in some distant place, and which would not admit of a moment's delay. Presently after, he would conceive his house to be on fire, and would hastily endeavour to rescue his property from the flames. Then he would fancy that his son was drowning, that he had twice sunk: he was prepared to plunge into the river to save him, as he floated for the last time: every moment appeared an hour until he rose. In this miserable state he continued till the 27th, when, with great perturbation, he suddenly ran into his room, threw himself on the bed, and in a few minutes expired. The head was opened twenty-four hours after death. The pericranium was but slightly adherent to the scull: the tunica arachnoidea, particularly where the hemispheres meet, was of a milky whiteness. Between this membrane, which was somewhat thickened, and the pia mater, there was a very large collection of water: the pia mater was inflamed: the veins of this membrane were enlarged beyond what I had ever before observed: there was a striking appearance of air in the veins: the medullary substance of the brain, when cut into, bled freely, and seemed spongy from the number and enlargement of its vessels: in the ventricles, which were of a natural capacity, there was about half an ounce of water: the brain was of a healthy consistence.

CASE XX.

M. L. a woman, aged thirty-eight, was admitted into the house, June 11, 1796. From the information of the people who had attended her, it appeared, that she had been disordered six weeks, and that the disease took place shortly after the death of her husband. At the first attack she was violent, but she soon became more calm. She conceived that the overseers of the parish, to which she belonged, meditated her destruction: afterwards she supposed them deeply enamoured of her, and that they were to decide their claims by a battle. During the time she continued in the hospital she was perfectly quiet, although very much deranged. She fancied that a young man, for whom she had formerly entertained a partiality, but who had been dead some years, appeared frequently at her bed-side, in a state of putrefaction, which left an abominable stench in her room. Soon after she grew suspicious, and became apprehensive of evil intentions in the people about her. She would frequently watch at her door, and, when asked the reason, replied that she was fully aware of a design, which had been formed, to put her secretly to death.—Under the influence of these opinions she continued to her death, which took place on February 8, 1797, in consequence of a violent rheumatic fever. She was opened twelve hours after death. There were two opake spots on the tunica arachnoidea: the pia mater was slightly inflamed: there was a general congestion of blood to the whole contents of the cranium: the consistence of the brain did not differ from what is found in a healthy state.

CASE XXI.

H. C. a woman, of about sixty-five years of age, had been admitted on the incurable establishment in the year 1788. I have not been able to collect any particulars of her former history. During the time I had an opportunity of seeing her, she continued in a very violent and irritable state: it was her custom to abuse every one who came near her. The greatest part of the day was passed in cursing the persons she saw about her; and when no one was near, she usually muttered some blasphemy to herself. She died of a fever on February 19, 1797, on the fourth day after the attack. She was opened two days after death. The tunica arachnoidea was, in many parts, without its natural transparency: the pia mater was generally suffused with blood, and its vessels were enlarged: the consistence of the brain was firm.

CASE XXII.

J. C. a man, aged fifty, was admitted into the hospital, August 6, 1796. It was stated that he had been disordered about three weeks, and that the disease had been induced by too great attention to business, and the want of sufficient rest. About four years before, he had been a patient, and was discharged uncured. He was an artful and designing man, and with great ingenuity once effected his escape from the hospital. His time was mostly passed in childish amusements, such as tearing pieces of paper and sticking them on the walls of his room, collecting rubbish and assorting it. However, when he conceived himself unobserved, he was intriguing with other patients, and instructing them in the means, by which they might escape. Of his disorder he seemed highly sensible, and appeared to approve so much of his confinement, that when his friends wished to have him released, he opposed it, except it should meet with my approbation; telling them, in my presence, that, although he might appear well to them, the medical people of the house were alone capable of judging of the actual state of his mind; yet I afterwards discovered, that he had instigated them to procure his enlargement, by a relation of the grossest falshoods and most unjust complaints. In April 1797, he was permitted to have a month's leave of absence, as he appeared tolerably well, and wished to maintain his family by his industry. For above three weeks of this time, he conducted himself in a very rational and orderly manner. The day preceding that, on which he was to have returned thanks, he appeared gloomy and suspicious, and felt a disinclination for work. The night was passed in a restless manner, but in the morning he seemed better, and proposed coming to the hospital to obtain his discharge. His wife having been absent for a few minutes from the room, found him, on her return, with his throat cut. He was re-admitted as a patient, and expressed great sorrow and penitence for what he had done; and said that it was committed in a moment of rashness and despair. After a long and minute examination, he bewrayed nothing incoherent in his discourse. His wound, from which it was stated that he had lost a large quantity of blood, was attended to by Mr. Crowther, the surgeon to the hospital. Every day he became more dispirited, and at last refused to speak. He died May 29th, about ten days after his re-admission. His head was opened two days after death. There were some slight opacities of the tunica arachnoidea, and the pia mater was a little inflamed: the other parts of the brain were in an healthy state, and its consistence natural.

CASE XXIII.

E. L. was a man, about seventy-eight years of age; had been admitted on the incurable establishment, January 3, 1767. By report, I have understood that he was formerly in the navy, and that his insanity was caused by a disappointment of some promotion which he expected. It was also said, that he was troublesome to some persons high in office, which rendered it necessary that he should be confined. At one time he imagined himself to be the king, and insisted on his crown. During the time I had an opportunity of knowing him, he conducted himself in a very gentlemanly manner. His disposition was remarkably placid, and I never remember him to have uttered an unkind or hasty expression. With the other patients he seldom held any conversation. His chief amusement was reading, and writing letters to the people of the house. Of his books he was by no means choice; he appeared to derive as much amusement from an old catalogue as from the most entertaining performance. His writings always contained directions for his release from confinement; and he never omitted his high titles of God's King, Holy Ghost, Admiral, and Physician. He died June 13, 1797, worn out with age. He was opened two days after death. The scull was thick and porous. There was a large quantity of water between the different membranes. The tunica arachnoidea was particularly opake: the veins seemed to contain air: in the medullary substance the vessels were very copious and much enlarged: the lateral ventricles contained two ounces of pellucid water: the consistence of the brain was natural.

It has been stated, by a gentleman of great accuracy, and whose situation affords him abundant opportunity of acquiring a knowledge of diseased appearances, that the fluid of hydrocephalus appears to be of the same nature with the water which is found in dropsy of the thorax and abdomen.[10] That this is generally the case, there can be no doubt, from the respectable testimony of the author of the Morbid Anatomy: but in three instances, where I submitted this fluid to experiment, it was incoagulable by acids and by heat; in all of them its consistence was not altered even by boiling. There was, however, a cloudiness produced; and, after the liquor had stood some time, a slight deposition of animal matter took place, which, prior to the application of heat or mineral acids, had been dissolved in the fluid. This liquor tinged green the vegetable blues; produced a copious deposition with nitrat of silver; and, on evaporation, afforded cubic crystals (nitrat of soda). From this examination it was inferred, that the water of the brain, collected in maniacal cases, contained a quantity of uncombined alkali and some common salt. What other substances may enter into its composition, from want of sufficient opportunity, I have not been enabled to determine.

CASE XXIV.

S. W. a woman, thirty-five years of age, was admitted into the hospital, June 3, 1797. It was stated that she had been one month disordered, and had never experienced any prior affection of the same kind. The disease was said to have been produced by misfortunes which had attended her family, and from frequent quarrels with those who composed it. She was in a truly melancholic state; she was lost to all the comforts of this life, and conceived herself abandoned for ever by God. She refused all food and medicines. In this wretched condition she continued until July 29th, when she lost the use of her right side. On the 30th she became lethargic, and continued so until her death, which happened on August the 3d. She was opened two days after death. There was a large collection of water between the different membranes of the brain, amounting at least to four ounces: the pia mater was very much inflamed, and was separable from the convolutions of the brain with unusual facility: the medullary substance was abundantly loaded with bloody points: the consistence of the brain was remarkably firm.

CASE XXV.

D. W. a man, about fifty-eight years of age, had been admitted upon the incurable establishment in 1789. He was of a violent and mischievous disposition, and had nearly killed one of the keepers at a private mad house previously to his admission into the hospital. At all times he was equally deranged respecting his opinions, although he was occasionally more quiet and tractable: these intervals were extremely irregular as to their duration and period of return. He was of a very constipated habit, and required large doses of cathartic medicines to procure stools. On August 3, 1797, he was in a very furious state; complained of costiveness, for which he took his ordinary quantity of opening physic, which operated as usual. On the same day he ate his dinner with a good appetite; but about six o'clock in the evening he was struck with hemiplegia, which deprived him completely of the use of his left side. He lay insensible of what passed about him, muttered constantly to himself, and appeared to be keeping up a kind of conversation. The pulse was feeble, but not oppressed or intermitting. He never had any stertor. He continued in this state until the 12th, when he died. He was opened twelve hours after death. There was some water between the tunica arachnoidea and pia mater: the former membrane was opake in many places; bearing the marks of former inflammation: in the veins of the membranes of the brain there was a considerable appearance of air, and they were likewise particularly charged with blood: the vessels of the medullary substance were numerous and enlarged. On opening the right lateral ventricle, which was much distended, it was found filled with dark and grumous blood; some had also escaped into the left, but in quantity inconsiderable when compared with what was contained in the other: the consistence of the brain was very soft.

CASE XXVI.

J. S. a man, forty-four years of age, was received into the hospital, June 24, 1797. He had been disordered nine months previous to his admission. His insanity was attributed to a violent quarrel, which had taken place with a young woman, to whom he was attached, as he shortly afterwards became sullen and melancholy.

During the time he remained in the house he seldom spoke, and wandered about like a forlorn person. Sometimes he would suddenly stop, and keep his eyes fixed on an object, and continue to stare at it for more than an hour together. Afterwards he became stupid, hung down his head, and drivelled like an ideot. At length he grew feeble and emaciated, his legs were swollen and œdematous, and on September 13th, after eating his dinner, he crawled to his room, where he was found dead about an hour afterwards. He was opened two days after death. The tunica arachnoidea had a milky whiteness, and was thickened. There was a considerable quantity of water between that membrane and the pia mater, which latter was loaded with blood: the lateral ventricles were very much enlarged, and contained, by estimation, about six ounces of transparent fluid: the brain was of its natural consistence.

CASE XXVII.

T. W. a man, thirty-eight years of age, was admitted into the house, May 16, 1795. He had then been disordered a year. His disease was stated to have arisen, from his having been defrauded, by two of his near relations, of some property, which he had accumulated by servitude. Having remained in the hospital the usual time of trial for cure, he was afterwards continued on the incurable establishment, in consequence of a strong determination he had always shewn, to be revenged on those people who had disposed of his property, and a declared intention of destroying himself. He was in a very miserable state, conceived that he had offended God, and that his soul was burning in Hell. Notwithstanding he was haunted with these dreadful imaginations, he acted with propriety upon most occasions. He took delight in rendering any assistance in his power to the people about the house, and waited on those who were sick, with a kindness that made him generally esteemed. At some period of his life he had acquired an unfortunate propensity to gaming, and whenever he had collected a few pence, he ventured them at cards. His losses were borne with very little philosophy, and the devil was always accused of some unfair interposition.

On September 14, 1797, he appeared jaundiced, the yellowness daily increased, and his depression of mind was more tormenting than ever. From the time he was first attacked by the jaundice he had a strong presentiment that he should die. Although he took the medicines which were ordered, as a mark of attention to those who prescribed them, he was firmly persuaded they could be of no service. The horror and anxiety he felt, was, he said, sufficient to kill him, independantly of the jaundice.

On the 20th he was drowsy, and on the following day died comatose. He was opened twenty-four hours after death. In some places the tunica arachnoidea was slightly opake: the pia mater was inflamed; and in the ventricles were found about two tea-spoons full of water tinged deeply yellow, and the vesicles of the plexus choroides were of the same colour: to the whole contents of the cranium there was a considerable congestion of blood: the consistence of the brain was natural: the liver was sound: the gall-bladder very much thickened, and contained a stone of the mulberry appearance, of a white colour. Another stone was also found in the duodenum.

CASE XXVIII.

R. B. a man, sixty-four years of age, was admitted into the hospital, September 2, 1797. He had then been disordered three months. It was also stated, that he had suffered an attack of this disease seven years before, which then continued about two months. His disorder had, both times, been occasioned by drinking spirituous liquors to excess. He was a person of liberal education, and had been occasionally employed as usher in a school, and at other times as a librarian and amanuensis. When admitted he was very noisy, and importunately talkative. During the greatest part of the day he was reciting passages from the Greek and Roman poets, or talking of his own literary importance. He became so troublesome to the other madmen, who were sufficiently occupied with their own speculations, that they avoided, and excluded him from the common room; so that he was, at last, reduced to the mortifying situation of being the sole auditor of his own compositions.

He conceived himself very nearly related to Anacreon, and possessed of the peculiar vein of that poet. He also fancied that he had discovered the longitude; and was very urgent for his liberation from the hospital, that he might claim the reward, to which his discovery was intitled. At length he formed schemes to pay off the national debt: these, however, so much bewildered him that his disorder became more violent than ever, and he was in consequence obliged to be confined to his room. He now, after he had remained two months in the house, was more noisy than before, and had little sleep. These exertions very much reduced him.

In the beginning of January, 1798, his conceptions were less distinct, and although his talkativeness continued, he was unable to conclude a single sentence. When he began to speak, his attention was diverted by the first object which caught his eye, or by any sound that struck him. On the 5th he merely muttered; on the 7th he lost the use of his right side, and became stupid and taciturn. In this state he continued until the 14th, when he had another fit; after which he remained comatose and insensible. On the following day he died. He was opened thirty-six hours after death. The pericranium adhered very loosely to the scull: the tunica arachnoidea was generally opake, and suffused with a brownish hue: a large quantity of water was contained between it and the pia mater: the contents of the cranium were unusually destitute of blood: there was a considerable quantity of water (perhaps four ounces) in the lateral ventricles, which were much enlarged: the consistence of the brain was very soft.

CASE XXIX.

E. T. a man, aged thirty years, was admitted a patient, July 23, 1796. The persons who attended, related, that he had been disordered eleven months, and that his insanity shortly supervened to a violent fever. It also appeared, from subsequent enquiries, that his mother had been affected with madness.

He was a very violent and mischievous patient, and possessed of great bodily strength and activity. Although confined, he contrived several times during the night to tear up the flooring of his cell; and had also detached the wainscot to a considerable extent, and loosened a number of bricks in the wall. When a new patient was admitted, he generally enticed him into his room, on pretence of being an old acquaintance, and, as soon as he came within his reach, immediately tore his clothes to pieces. He was extremely dexterous with his feet, and frequently took off the hats of those who were near him with his toes, and destroyed them with his teeth. After he had dined he generally bit to pieces a thick wooden bowl, in which his food was served, on the principle of sharpening his teeth against the next meal. He once bit out the testicles of a living cat, because the animal was attached to some person who had offended him. Of his disorder he appeared to be very sensible; and after he had done any mischief, always blamed the keepers for not securing him so, as to have prevented it. After he had continued a year in the hospital he was retained as an incurable patient. He died February 17, 1798, in consequence of a tumor of the neck. He was opened two days after death. The tunica arachnoidea was generally opake, and of a milky whiteness: the vessels of the pia mater were turgid, and its veins contained a quantity of air; about an ounce of water was contained in the lateral ventricles: the consistence of the brain was unusually firm, and possessed of considerable elasticity: it is the only instance of this nature which has fallen under my observation.

CASE XXX.

T. G. a man, about fifty-five years of age, was admitted into the hospital, January 20, 1798. It was stated, that he had been disordered a year and half, and that his madness arose from repeated intoxication. Having set fire to several hay-stacks, and committed frequent depredations on the neighbouring farmers, it had been found necessary to confine him in the county goal. His behaviour in this situation marked the cunning and malignity of his mind, so that he was always attempting some mischief either by violence or stratagem.

When brought to the hospital he conducted himself with propriety and order, and appeared to be in a state of recovery. On the second of May he was attacked with a diarrhœa which daily encreased, notwithstanding the medicines employed for its removal. His mind became violently agitated from the commencement of the diarrhœa, and it was found proper to secure him. On the 8th, dysenteric symptoms appeared, which continued to the 13th, when he died.

Appearances on Dissection.

The head was opened twenty-four hours after death. The pericranium was loosely attached to the scull, and the dura mater adhered but slightly to the internal surface of the cranium; there was a considerable quantity of water between the dura mater and tunica arachnoidea, this latter membrane (especially where the hemispheres meet) was of a milky whiteness, and generally so in the course of the veins of the pia mater. The glandulæ Pacchioni were very large and numerous. Between the tunica arachnoidea and pia mater there was much water; and from the lateral ventricles, which were uncommonly enlarged and distended, eight ounces of fluid were collected: the infundibulum was remarkably large: the membrane lining the cavity of the lateral ventricles had its veins very turgid: the consistence of the brain was softer than natural.

The fluid obtained from the brain in this case being very pellucid and abundant, it was submitted to some chemical tests in order to ascertain its composition.

An attempt of this kind had been made before; (vide Case 23) the present may be considered a small addition to our knowledge of this fluid, though by no means a satisfactory developement of its materials, according to the severity and precision of modern analysis.[11]

Tincture of Galls,	produced a white precipitate in moderate quantity.
Lime Water,	afforded a considerable quantity of a white precipitate, which was redissolved without effervescence by muriatic acid.
Solution of Sulphat of Copper.	A drop of this solution added to two drams of the brain fluid tinged it with a pretty deep blue.

The presence of animal matter is inferred from the deposition produced by infusion of galls.

The precipitation by lime-water indicates the phosphoric acid.

And it appears from the blue tinge given to the fluid by the sulphat of copper, that ammonia or some of its combinations was contained.

As it occurred on many former trials, there was no coagulation by heat; a slight sediment fell, after boiling some minutes.

As this patient remained in the hospital from the middle of January to the beginning of May, in a state perfectly tranquil, and without the appearance of disarrangement of mind, it is improbable that a so great enlargement of the ventricles, and accumulation of water, could have taken place within the short space of two weeks, it is therefore most likely that the greatest part of this fluid had been previously collected.

It may be conjectured that a very gradual accumulation of water (although the quantity be at last considerable) would not affect the sensorium so as a sudden secretion of fluid; or, that a quantity, which at one time had occasioned great disturbance, would by habit become less inconvenient.

We are not well informed, but there is reason to believe, that gradual pressure on the brain, will not occasion those serious symptoms which a sudden pressure would excite.

CASE XXXI.

H. K. a woman, aged thirty, was admitted into the hospital, October 15, 1796. She had then been mad about four months, and her disorder was stated to have supervened on the birth of a child. From subsequent enquiry it was ascertained that her mother had been insane, and that her elder sister had been similarly affected; but from the best information it did not appear that her brothers (she had two) had ever been visited with this calamity.

Previously to her admission she had frequently attempted to destroy herself, and had also endeavoured to take away the life of her husband. In the hospital she was extremely violent; supposed her neighbours had conspired to take away her liberty, and became jealous of her husband: she was often naming some female of her acquaintance who had artfully ensnared his affections, and whom he had decked out in her best apparel: she breathed revenge when she should return home, and seemed much delighted with the idea of destroying these favourites, when they were dressed for some excursion with her husband.

She had understood that a year was the extent of time that persons were detained in the hospital, and conceived she should be liberated when it had elapsed, to put her menaces into execution. Her disorder being of a dangerous tendency she was retained in the hospital after the period of probation. When she found the hope of gratifying her revenge frustrated, by being kept beyond the time of her expectation, she began to pine away, her appetite diminished, and a cough, with copious expectoration and hectic fever supervened. During the whole period of her bodily disease, she would never acknowledge herself to be ill, and the violence of her mental disorder was unabated. She died of Phthisis Pulmonalis, April 1st, 1798.

The head was opened twenty four hours after her decease. The tunica arachnoidea was in many places opake; the pia mater was highly inflamed, and loaded with blood, and a considerable quantity of water was contained between it and the former membrane. The ventricles were enlarged, but contained scarcely any fluid. The other parts of the brain were healthy, and its consistence was natural.

It is a common opinion, that Phthisis Pulmonalis is frequently suspended by the supervention of mania; medical books abound with such accounts, and some persons have supposed it difficult, if not impossible, for these diseases to co-exist. It is not my intention to dispute the accuracy of such relations, nor to question the power which Mania may possess in arresting the progress of Phthisis Pulmonalis, but, to state that the converse does not obtain; and, that whatever obligations may be due from Phthisis to Mania, the compliment has not been returned. From my own experience I can affirm, that insane persons are as liable to Phthisis Pulmonalis as others, that numbers of them die of that disease; and that I never saw any abatement of the maniacal symptoms through the progress of consumption.

CASE XXXII.

J. P. aged 57, was admitted into the hospital, January 19, 1799; he was stated to have been insane about three weeks, and that his disorder came on shortly after the death of his master, in whose service he had continued many years, and to whom he was much attached. He had been in the hospital three times before, and had each time been discharged well. His disorder usually recurred every seven or eight years. His father also had been maniacal about the middle period of life, but never recovered. When admitted he was very talkative, although his natural character was reserved. He endeavoured to explain his meaning with superior correctness, and sought to define every subject, however trifling, with a tedious minuteness; but, upon religion and politics, the Scylla and Charybdis of human discussion, he was pertinacious and intollerant. This dictatorial manner and stubbornness of opinion, not being capable of producing the relations of peace and amity with other philosophers, equally obstinate, and whose principles had been matured by long confinement, it became necessary to shut him up in his cell. During the period of his seclusion, nothing very incoherent escaped from him; every thing he said was within the sphere of possibility. His fastidiousness rendered him unhappy: he acknowledged the food which was brought him to be good, but he conceived it might have been better. The cathartic medicine, which was administered to him, he confessed had answered the purpose, but its taste was most nauseous, and he had never before been so severely griped. He ornamented his person and apartment in a very whimsical manner: latterly he tore his clothes because he suspected the taylor had deceived him in the materials. After this he continued naked until the beginning of March, when he appeared more composed, and sensible of the state he had been in. On the morning of the 12th, when the keeper opened his cell, he was speechless; his mouth drawn to the right side, and so feeble that he could not support himself. A cathartic medicine was given, and sinapisms were applied to the feet and legs. In the evening he was much recovered, his speech had returned, and he was able to move himself. He was visited again at midnight, when he appeared still better. In the morning it was evident that he had experienced another attack, his mouth was drawn aside; he was stupid, and died within half an hour. The head was opened on the following day. The tunica arachnoidea was in some places slightly opake. The pia mater was inflamed, but not to any considerable degree. There was no water between any of the membranes. The ventricles were of a natural capacity, and did not contain any fluid. There was no extravasation in any part of the substance of the cerebrum or cerebellum. Excepting the slight inflammation of the pia mater, the brain had a very healthy appearance; its consistence was firm; the scull was unusually thick. I regret, from a promise which had been made to the friends, of inspecting the head only, that the thoracic and abdominal viscera were not examined.

This history has been related to shew, that although the patient died with those symptoms, which indicate pressure on the brain, as loss of speech, the mouth being drawn aside, stupor and insensibility; yet the brain did not afford the same appearances, on dissection, as have been usually detected in such cases. The following relation is an additional example of the same fact:

CASE XXXIII.

N. B. He had been many years in the hospital as an incurable patient; his mother was known to have been maniacal; his two brothers and his sister have been insane. His eldest son, on taking a very small quantity of fermented liquor, becomes frantic, and its effects continue much longer than on persons in general. During this patient's confinement, he was, as far as could be ascertained, completely in his senses; this induced the medical persons of the hospital, on two or three occasions, to give him leave of absence, that he might return on trial to his wife and family; but, in a few hours after he came home, he felt uneasy, and found himself bewitched at all points: the devil and his imps had pre-occupied the best places in the house; he became very turbulent, and also jealous of his wife, and was obliged to be returned to the hospital. As he found his home so beset with difficulties he resolved that he would never enter it again. During eight years that I was acquainted with him I never discovered the least insanity in his actions or conversation. He was perfectly sensible that his intellects were disordered whenever he returned to his family. His wife and children frequently visited him in Bethlem, and he always conducted himself affectionately towards them. About 14 months before his death he laboured under a severe dysentery, which continued six weeks, and left him in a very reduced state, with œdematous legs, and incipient dropsy of the abdomen. On his recovery from these symptoms he became troubled with fits; they appeared to be such as a medical person would have termed apoplectic. After the attack, no symptoms of paralysis remained, nor did he experience the fatigue and exhaustion, or fall into a profound sleep, which usually accompanies Epilepsy. On October 10th, 1802, being then in a pretty good state of health, he fell down, and expired in a few minutes. He was about sixty-five years of age. On examination of the head after death, there was a considerable determination of blood to the brain; but there was no extravasation of that fluid, nor any collection of water: the brain and its membranes had a healthy appearance, and its consistence was natural. The heart was sound, and the abdominal viscera were not conspicuously diseased.

CASE XXXIV.

J. P. a man, aged thirty, was admitted into the hospital, October 18th, 1800. It was then deposed, by the persons who brought him, that he had been for eight months in a melancholic state; but they were unable to assign any circumstances, which preceded his disorder, as a cause of his disease. He had a large tumor on the throat which extended backward to the neck, principally on the left side; the increase of this swelling, they alledged, had much alarmed him, at the commencement of his melancholic attack. During the time he was the subject of my observation, he was in a very mopish and stupid state; if spoken to, he would sometimes give a short answer, but ordinarily he took no notice of those who addressed him. Some days he would walk slowly in the less frequented part of the building; frequently he sat down for some hours in a corner. His appetite was good, he ate the food which was brought him, but never took the trouble to go for it, when serving out. In this state he continued until April 2d, when he became more stupid, and could not be made to rise from his bed. He did not appear to be in any pain, nor was he at all convulsed. His bowels were regular. On the 5th he became comatose, and on the 9th he died.

Appearances on Dissection.

There was an excessive determination of blood to the brain, and the pia mater was highly inflamed. On the inferior part of the middle lobe of the brain, there was a gangrene of considerable extent, together with a quantity of very fœtid purulent matter.

This is the only instance of a gangrenous state of the brain which has fallen under my observation.

CASE XXXV.

T. C. This person had remained many years in the hospital on the incurable establishment. He had been a schoolmaster at Warrington in Lancashire, and was a man of acuteness and extensive mathematical learning. As he became very furious on the attack of his maniacal disorder, he was placed in the Lunatic Asylum at Manchester, where he killed the person who had the care of him, by stabbing him in the back with a knife.

The following is the account he gave me of that transaction, and which I immediately committed to paper; as it conveys a serious and important lesson to those who are about the persons of the insane.

"He that would govern others, first should be
The master of himself, richly indu'd
With depth of understanding, height of courage."
Massinger's Bondman, Act I. *Scene* 3.

It ought to be more generally understood that a madman seldom forgets the coercion he has undergone, and that he never forgives an indignity.

"The man whom I stabbed richly deserved it. He behaved to me with great violence and cruelty, he degraded my nature as a human being; he tied me down, handcuffed me, and confined my hands much higher than my head, with a leathern thong: he stretched me on a bed of torture. After some days he released me. I gave him warning, for I told his wife I would have justice of him. On her communicating this to him, he came to me in a furious passion, threw me down, dragg'd me through the court-yard, thumped on my breast, and confined me in a dark and damp cell. Not liking this situation, I was induced to play the hypocrite. I pretended extreme sorrow for having threatened him, and by an affectation of repentance, prevailed on him to release me. For several days I paid him great attention, and lent him every assistance. He seemed much pleased with the flattery, and became very friendly in his behaviour towards me.—Going one day into the kitchen, where his wife was busied, I saw a knife; (this was too great a temptation to be resisted;) I concealed it, and carried it about me. For some time afterwards the same friendly intercourse was maintained between us; but, as he was one day unlocking his garden door, I seized the opportunity, and plunged the knife up to the hilt in his back."—He always mentioned this circumstance with peculiar triumph, and his countenance (the most cunning and malignant I ever beheld) became highly animated at the conclusion of the story.

During the time he was in Bethlem Hospital he most ingeniously formed a stiletto out of a mop-nail; it was an elaborate contrivance, and had probably been the work of several months. It was rendered extremely sharp and polished, by whetting on a small pebble; it was fixed into a handle, and had a wooden sheath made from the mop-stick. This instrument he carried in his left breeches pocket, his right hand grasping the hilt. As I always found him in that posture when I visited him, I suspected he had some concealed implement of mischief, and therefore employed a convalescent patient to watch him through the key-hole of his door. This person saw him with the weapon, and also ascertaining the distance at which he could use it.

The instrument was taken from him by surprise. When he found he was prevented from executing his purpose, he roared out the most horrid imprecations; he cursed the Almighty for creating him, and more especially for having given him the form of a human being, and he wished to go to Hell that he might not be disgraced by an association with the Deity.

He had an uniform and implacable aversion to the officers and servants of the hospital; he said he courted their hatred for their curse was a blessing. He seldom answered a question but some impiety was contained in the reply. An indifferent person remarking that it was a bad day, he immediately retorted, "Sir, did you ever know God make a good one?" Although the whole of the day, and the greatest part of the night, were consumed in pouring forth abuse and coining new blasphemies; yet there were some few patients for whom he professed a friendship, and with whom he conversed in a mild and civil way: this confidence had been obtained by the compliments they had addressed to him on the score of his understanding, of which he entertained a very high opinion. At one time he conceived himself to be the Messiah, at another, that he was Mr. Adam, the architect; and that he was shortly to go to America in order to build the new Jerusalem in Philadelphia.

About six months before his death he complained of pain in his stomach, and said he felt as if he had no intestines. His appetite diminished, and he became melancholic.

The scene now began to alter; he had a presentiment that his time in this world would be short, and he dreaded the change: no hope arose, no consolation could cheer him; he became daily more emaciated and despairing until he died, which took place August 27, 1801; he appeared to be about seventy years of age.

On opening the head, the pericranium was scarcely adherent. This membrane being removed, blood oozed freely from the parietal bones. There was a large accumulation of water between the dura mater and tunica arachnoidea; when this was let out the dura mater became flaccid, and seemed to hang loose on the brain. On the left posterior lobe of the cerebrum there was a large quantity of a milky fluid, between the tunica arachnoidea and pia mater, giving the appearance of a vesication; and in that place there was a depression or cavity formed in the convolutions of the brain. The convolutions were so strongly and distinctly marked, that they resembled the intestines of a child. The lateral ventricles were but little distended, and did not contain much water. The head was not particularly loaded with blood, nor were the bloody points, in the medullary substance, very abundant. The brain was of a natural consistence. There was no disease in the stomach, intestines, or liver. The body was opened about six hours after his death.

CASE XXXVI.

B. S. a man, generally noticed by those who have visited Bethlem hospital a few years ago. It was said, that an attachment to a young woman, who slighted his addresses, was the cause of his becoming insane. He was considered a very dangerous lunatic, and for many years was confined to his cell. In this situation he employed himself in the manufacture of straw baskets and table mats. The desire of money was the leading feature of his mind, and the whole of his energies were devoted to its acquisition; nor was he at all scrupulous as to the means, by which he attained his object. Although repeatedly assured that he would never be liberated, he disbelieved such information, and was persuaded, when he had acquired a sum sufficient to purchase a horse and cart, filled with higler's ware, that he should be released. The idea of becoming a trader, on so large a scale, stimulated him to constant occupation. He employed several lunatic journeymen to plat the straw for him, but they were poorly rewarded. He generally chose for his workmen such as were chained, and could not come personally to insist on the reward of their labour. He commonly pretended that the platting was badly performed, and consequently unsaleable; sometimes he would protest that he had settled with them, but that they were too mad to recollect it; and if at any time he did pay them, it was in bad coin. For many years he was unrivalled in this trade, and, by every species of fraud, had amassed nearly sufficient to set his plans afloat: when an unfortunate event took place, which considerably reduced his capital. He had always a propensity to game, which, from his skill and dexterity in cheating, was generally attended with success; but in this science he was once over-matched. An insane soldier, an ingenious man, became his intimate friend, and finding him possessed of some money proposed a game at cards. The result was deeply disastrous to the artificer in straw, who endeavoured to evade the payment; but his friend stated it to be a debt of honor; and besides he was a very powerful man, of a stern aspect, and not to be trifled with; he was therefore compelled to tell down at once the slow accumulation of several years. It was intended to make the soldier restore the property, but he, conceiving that he had already derived sufficient benefit from the hospital, went away in the night, without the formalities of a regular discharge.

To fill up the measure of his misfortunes, when Hatfield, the maniac who shot at his Majesty in the theatre, was brought to Bethlem, he, in conjunction with a contriving cobbler, established a rival manufactory, which shortly eclipsed the fabric of the old school, and by superior taste rendered his further exertions unnecessary.

It is natural to suppose, that no great cordiality could exist between persons, where the prosperity of one had been established on the ruin of the other. Frequent altercations arose, and much offensive language was exchanged. At length the patience of the original dealer was exhausted, and, in collecting his force to give his opponent a blow, he fell down and instantly expired.—He was about fifty-eight years of age.

Some of his habits and opinions were extremely singular; he believed that all occurrences were regulated by witches: prosperity was to be attributed to the good witches having obtained the mastery; and when bad witches gained the ascendancy, misfortunes arose. When the latter were at work he supposed himself in possession of a power to frighten and disperse them, and this was effected by a peculiar noise he made. It is probable he might have laboured under indigestion, for immediately after he had eaten his dinner, he sent forth a dreadful howl, which he continued for about ten minutes: but his great terror was a thunder storm; when this occurred, he took a very active part, and brought the whole force of his lungs to bear upon the enemy. A cat was supposed to have a natural antipathy to bad witches, she could smell them at a distance; for which reason he always domesticated an animal of that kind to sleep in his cell.

When his head was opened, the dura mater was very easily separable from the scull; upon puncturing this membrane a considerable quantity of blood flowed from the opening; and there was a copious extravasation of this fluid between the membranes of the brain: but the most remarkable circumstance was, that the tunica arachnoidea was so thickened, that it exceeded the dura mater on an accurate comparison. The pia mater was loaded with blood, and its vessels were enlarged. The brain and its cavities were sound and natural.

CASE XXXVII.

R. B. This man had been many years an incurable patient, and it was supposed that jealousy of his wife had been the cause of his madness, although it appeared from very respectable testimony that he had no real grounds for such suspicion. During eight years, (the period he was subject to my observation,) he was mostly in a very furious state, and obliged to be strictly confined. His mischeivous disposition was manifested on every occasion; he would hurl the bowl, in which his food was served, against those who passed his cell; and when his hands were secured he would kick, bite, or throw his head into the stomachs of those who came near him. He entertained a constant aversion to his keeper, whom he suspected to be connected with his wife. His life was miserably divided between furious paroxysms and melancholic languor, and there was great uncertainty in the duration of these states. He has been known to continue ten months in the highest degree of violence, and relapse into the same state after a few days passed in tranquil depression. There was one circumstance which never failed to produce a relapse, however quietly he might have conducted himself, this was a visit from any of his family, and a very striking instance occurred. From May, 1799, to September, 1800, he had every appearance of being perfectly recovered: he was, in consequence, allowed additional comforts, and treated as a convalescent. At this time he was visited by his son, who, after many hours conversation with him, was persuaded that he had perfectly recovered his intellects; and he expressed himself astonished at his father's accurate recollection of particulars which might be supposed to have been obliterated from his mind. This dutiful visit and affectionate intercourse produced unpleasant consequences. The numerous enquiries which the patient had made, furnished him with materials for reflexion. On the departure of his son he began to detect mismanagement in his affairs, and improprieties in the conduct of his family: he was very talkative, and became impatient to return home. The following day he had a wildness in his eyes, spoke fast, and appeared busy: before the evening he was so irritable and disobedient that it became necessary to confine him. From this time he continued in the most furious condition, singing and vociferating the greatest part of the night, until January 2d, 1801, when he became suddenly calm, complained of extreme debility, and said he should die in a few hours. He gave very proper answers to the questions which were asked him, but complained of the fatigue which talking induced. On the next morning he expired. He was sixty-eight years of age. The head was opened two days after his death. The tunica arachnoidea was in many places opake, and considerably thickened. There was a small quantity of limpid water between this membrane and the pia mater. When the medullary substance was cut into, there oozed from many points a quantity of dark blood, indeed the whole head was loaded with venous blood. The lateral ventricles were considerably enlarged and filled with water—four ounces were collected. The internal carotid arteries were much enlarged, and when divided, did not collapse, but remained open, as arteries in the other parts of the body. The consistence of the brain was doughy.

CHAP. IV.

CASES OF INSANE CHILDREN.

IN the month of March, 1799, a female child, three years and a quarter old, was brought to the hospital for medical advice. She was in good bodily health, and born of sane and undiseased parents. The mother, who attended, stated that her husband's parents and her own had never been in the slightest degree afflicted with mania, but that she had a brother who was born an ideot. She related that her child, until the age of two years and a half, was perfectly well, of ordinary vivacity, and of promising talents; when she was inoculated for the small pox. Severe convulsions ushered in the disease, and a delirium continued during its course. The eruption was of the mild kind, and the child was not marked with the pustules. From the termination of the small-pox to the above date, (nine months) the child continued in an insane state. Previously to the small-pox, she could articulate many words, and use them correctly for the things they signified: but since that time she completely forgot her former acquisitions, nor ever attempted to imitate a significant sound. Whatever she wished to perform, she effected with promptitude and facility. She appeared anxious to possess every thing she saw, and cried if she experienced any disappointment; and on these occasions she would bite, or express her anger by kicking or striking. Her appetite was voracious, and she would devour any thing that was given to her, without discrimination; as fat, raw animal food, or tainted meat. To rake out the fire with her fingers was a favourite amusement, nor was she deterred from having frequently burned them. She passed her urine and fæces in any place without restraint; but she could retain a considerable quantity of the former before she discharged it. Some cathartic remedies were ordered for her, with an emetic occasionally, and she was brought to the hospital every fortnight, but she did not appear in any degree amended. On June 22 she was admitted a patient, and continued in the hospital until the middle of October, when she was attacked with an eruptive fever, and consequently discharged. During this time little progress was made, although considerable pains were bestowed. She became more cunning, and her taste appeared improved. The cathartic medicine, which she drank at first without reluctance, became afterwards highly disgusting, and when she saw the basket which contained it, she endeavoured to escape and hide herself. To particular persons she was friendly, and felt an aversion to others. She was sensible of the authority of the nurse who attended her, and understood by the tone of her voice whether she were pleased or offended. The names of some things she appeared to comprehend, although they were extremely few; when the words, dinner, cakes, orange, and some more were mentioned, she smiled, and appeared in expectation of receiving them. By great attention and perseverance on the part of the nurse, she was brought to evacuate her fæces and urine in a night stool.

After the elapse of three years I was informed that the child had made no intellectual progress.

W. H. a boy, nearly seven years of age, was admitted into the Hospital, June 8th, 1799. His mother, who frequently visited him, related the following particulars respecting his case.—She said that, within a month of being delivered of this child, she was frightened by a man in the street, who rudely put his hand on her abdomen. When the child was born it was subject to startings, and became convulsed on any slight indisposition. When a year old, he suffered much with the measles: and afterwards had a mild kind of inoculated small-pox. At this age she thought the child more lively than usual, and that he slept less than her other children had done. At two years, the mother perceived he could not be controled, and therefore frequently corrected him.

There was a tardiness in the developement of his physical powers. He was fifteen months old before he had a tooth, and unable to go alone at two years and a half: his mind was equally slow; he had arrived at his fourth year before he began to speak; and, when in his fifth, he had not made a greater proficiency in language than generally may be observed in children between two and three years. When admitted into the hospital, he wept at being separated from his mother, but his grief was of very short continuance. He was placed on the female side, and seemed highly delighted with the novelty of the scene: every object excited his curiosity, but he did not pause or dwell on any. He was constantly in action, and rapidly examined the different apartments of the building. To the patients in general he behaved with great insolence—he kicked and spat at them, and distorted his face in derision; but, on the appearance of the nurse, he immediately desisted, and assured her he was a very good boy. Great, but ineffectual, pains were taken, to make him understand the nature of truth,—he could never be brought to confess any mischief he had committed, and always took refuge in the convenient shelter of a lie. In a short time he acquired a striking talent for mimickry, and imitated many of the patients in their insane manners; he generally selected, for his models, those who were confined, as he could practise from such with impunity.

In about three months he had added considerably to his stock of language, but, unluckily, he had selected his expressions from those patients who were addicted to swearing and obscene conversation. To teach him the letters of the alphabet had many times been endeavoured, but always without success; the attempt uniformly disgusted him: he was not to be stimulated by coaxing or coercion; his mind was too excursive, to submit to the painful toil of recording elementary sounds; but it may rather be inferred that he did not possess a sufficient power of attention to become acquainted with arbitrary characters.

He was in good health, his pulse and bowels were regular, and his appetite was keen, but not voracious. One circumstance struck me, as very peculiar, in this boy,—he appeared to have very incorrect ideas of distance: he would frequently stretch out his hand, to grasp objects considerably beyond his reach, but this referred principally to height: he would endeavour to pluck out a nail from the ceiling, or snatch at the moon. In October he became unwell, and, at the mother's request, was discharged from the hospital.

In September 1805, I again saw the boy: he was then thirteen years of age, had grown very tall, and appeared to be in good health. He recollected me immediately, and mentioned the words, school Moorfields, nasty physic. On meeting with some of the female patients, he perfectly remembered them, and seemed for the moment, much pleased at the renewal of the acquaintance. By this time, he had made comparatively, a great progress in language; he knew the names of ordinary things, and was able to tell correctly the street in which he resided, and the number of his house. His mother informed me that he was particularly fond of going to church, although he was unable to comprehend the purpose for which he went: when there, he conducted himself with great order and decorum, but was disposed to remain after the congregation had dispersed. To shew how little he understood, why he frequented a place of worship: his mother once took him to church on Sacrament-sunday, and fearful of disturbing the persons assembled, by compelling him to return home, allowed him to be a spectator of those solemn administrations. The only reflexion he made on the subject, but in disjointed expressions, was, that he thought it extremely hard, that the ladies and gentlemen should eat rolls and drink gin, and never ask him to partake. In his person he was clean, and dressed himself with neatness. Having been taught when in the hospital to use a bowl for his necessary occasions, he obstinately continued the same practice when he returned home, and could never be persuaded to retire to the closet of convenience; but the business did not terminate here, when he had evacuated his intestines into the bowl he never failed to paint the room with its contents. To watch other boys when they were playing, or to observe the progress of mischief, gave him great satisfaction: but he never joined them, nor did he ever become attached to any one of them. Of his mother he appeared excessively fond, and he was constantly caressing her: but in his paroxysms of fury he felt neither awe nor tenderness, and on two occasions he threw a knife at her. Although equally ignorant of letters, as when discharged from the hospital, he took great delight in having gilt books; indeed every thing splendid attracted his attention, but more especially soldiers and martial music. He retained several tunes, and was able to whistle them very correctly. The day on which I last saw him his mind was completely occupied with soldiers; when questions were put to him, if he answered them it was little to the purpose, generally he did not notice them, but turned round to his mother and enquired about the soldiers.

The defect of this lad's mind, appeared to be a want of continued attention to things, in order to become acquainted with their nature; and he possessed less curiosity than other children, which serves to excite such attention: and this will in some degree explain, why he had never acquired any knowledge of things in a connected manner. His sentences were short, and he employed no particles to join them together. Although he was acquainted with the names of many things, and also with expressions which characterize passion, he applied them in an insulated way. For instance, if a shower fell, he would look up and say, "rains;" or when fine, "sun shines." When in the street he would pull his mother, to arrest her attention, and point to objects, as a fine horse, or a big dog; when he returned home he would repeat what had attracted his notice, but always speaking of himself in the third person. "Billy see fine horse, big dog, &c."[12] Of circumstances boldly impressed, or reiterated by habit, his memory was retentive, but as his attention was only roused by striking appearances, or loud intonations, ordinary occurrences passed by unobserved.

In the month of July 1803, my opinion was requested respecting a young gentleman, ten years of age, who was sent here, accompanied by a kind and decent young man, to take care of him. Previously to his arrival I had corresponded respecting his case with a very learned and respectable physician in the country, under whose care the boy had been placed. From the information furnished by this gentleman, and that which was collected from the keeper, I believe the former history of his case is correctly given.

The parents are persons of sound mind, and they do not remember any branches of their respective families to have been (in any manner) disordered in their intellects. The subject of the present relation was their eldest son; the second child was of a disposition remarkably mild; and the youngest, a boy, about two years and a half, was distinguished by the irritability and impatience of his temper.

At the age of two years, the subject of the present relation, became so mischievous and uncontroulable, that he was sent from home to be nursed by his aunt. In this situation, at the request of his parents, and with the concurrence of his relation, he was indulged in every wish, and never corrected for any perverseness or impropriety of conduct. Thus he continued until he was nearly nine years old, the creature of volition and the terror of the family. At the suggestion of the physician, whom I have before mentioned, and who was the friend of his parents: a person was appointed to watch over him. It being the opinion of the doctor that the case originated in over indulgence and perverseness; a different system of management was adopted. The superintendant was ordered to correct him for each individual impropriety. At this time the boy would neither dress nor undress himself, though capable of doing both; when his hands were at liberty, he tore his clothes: he broke every thing that was presented to him, or which came within his reach, and frequently refused to take food. He gave answers only to such questions as pleased him, and acted in opposition to every direction. The superintendant exercised this plan for several months, but perhaps not to the extent laid down; for it may be presumed, that after a a few flagellations his humanity prevailed over the medical hypothesis. When he became the subject of my own observation, he was of a very healthy appearance, and his head was well formed; this was also the opinion of several gentlemen, distinguished for their anatomical knowledge, to whom the boy was presented. His tongue was unusually thick, though his articulation was perfectly distinct. His countenance was decidedly maniacal.[13] His stature, for his age, was short, but he was well compacted, and possessed great bodily strength. Although his skin was smooth and clear, it was deficient in its usual sensibility; he bore the whip and the cane with less evidence of pain than other boys. Another circumstance convinced me of this fact. During the time he resided in London he was troubled with a boil on his leg; various irritating applications were made to the tumor, and the dressings were purposely taken off with less nicety than usual, yet he never complained. His pulse was natural, and his bowels were regular. His appetite was good, but not inordinate, and he bore the privation of food for a considerable time without uneasiness. Although he slept soundly, he often awoke as if suddenly alarmed, and he seemed to require a considerable duration of sleep.

He had a very retentive memory, and had made as great proficiency in speech as the generality of boys of his own age. Few circumstances appeared to give him pleasure, but he would describe very correctly any thing which had delighted him. As he wanted the power of continued attention, and was only attracted by fits and starts, it may be naturally supposed he was not taught letters, and still less that he would copy them. He had been several times to school, and was the hopeless pupil of many masters, distinguished for their patience and rigid discipline; it may therefore be concluded, that from these gentlemen, he had derived all the benefits which could result from privations to his stomach, and from the application of the rod to the more delicate parts of his skin.

On the first interview I had with him, he contrived, after two or three minutes acquaintance, to break a window and tear the frill of my shirt. He was an unrelenting foe to all china, glass, and crockery ware, whenever they came within his reach he shivered them instantly. In walking the street, the keeper was compelled to take the wall, as he uniformly broke the windows if he could get near them, and this operation he performed so dextrously, and with such safety to himself, that he never cut his fingers. To tear lace and destroy the finer textures of female ornament, seemed to gratify him exceedingly, and he seldom walked out without finding an occasion of indulging this propensity. He never became attached to any inferior animal, a benevolence so common to the generality of children: to these creatures his conduct was that of the brute: he oppressed the feeble, and avoided the society of those more powerful than himself. Considerable practice had taught him that he was the cat's master, and whenever this luckless animal approached him he plucked out its whiskers with wonderful rapidity; to use his own language, "*I must have her beard off.*" After this operation, he commonly threw the creature on the fire, or through the window. If a little dog came near him he kicked it, if a large one he would not notice it. When he was spoken to, he usually said, "I do not choose to answer." When he perceived any one who appeared to observe him attentively, he always said, "Now I will look unpleasant." The usual games of children afforded him no amusement; whenever boys were at play he never joined them: indeed, the most singular part of his character was, that he appeared incapable of forming a friendship with any one: he felt no considerations for sex, and would as readily kick or bite a girl as a boy. Of any kindness shewn him, he was equally insensible; he would receive an orange as a present, and afterwards throw it in the face of the donor.

To the man who looked after him, he appeared to entertain something like an attachment: when this person went out of the room, and pretended that he would go away, he raised a loud outcry, and said, "what will become of me, if he goes away; I like him, for he carries the cane which makes me a good boy:" but it is much to be doubted, whether he really bore an affection for his keeper; the man seemed to be of a different opinion, and said, when he grew older he should be afraid to continue with him, as he was persuaded the boy would destroy him, whenever he found the means and opportunity.

Of his own disorder he was sometimes sensible: he would often express a wish to die, for he said, "God had not made him like other children;" and when provoked, he would threaten to destroy himself.

During the time he remained here, I conducted him through the hospital, and pointed out to him several patients who were chained in their cells; he discovered no fear or alarm; and when I shewed him a mischievous maniac who was more strictly confined than the rest, he said, with great exultation, "this would be the right place for me." Considering the duration of his insanity, and being ignorant of any means by which he was likely to recover, he returned to his friends, after continuing a few weeks in London.

CHAP. V.

CAUSES OF INSANITY.

WHEN patients are admitted into Bethlem Hospital, an enquiry is always made of the friends who accompany them, respecting the cause supposed to have occasioned their insanity.

It will be readily conceived, that there must be great uncertainty attending the information we are able to procure upon this head: and even from the most accurate accounts, it would be difficult to pronounce, that the circumstances which are related to us, have actually produced the effect. The friends and relatives of patients are, upon many occasions, very delicate concerning this point, and cautious of exposing their frailties or immoral habits: and when the disease is connected with the family, they are oftentimes still more reserved in disclosing the truth.

Fully aware of the incorrect statement, frequently made concerning these causes, I have been at no inconsiderable pains to correct or confirm the first information, by subsequent enquiries.

The causes which I have been enabled most certainly to ascertain, may be divided into Physical and Moral.[14]

Under the first, are comprehended repeated intoxication: blows received upon the head; fever, particularly when attended with delirium; mercury, largely and injudiciously administered; cutaneous eruptions repelled, and the suppression of periodical or occasional discharges and secretions; hereditary disposition, and paralytic affections.

By the second class of causes, which have been termed *moral*, are meant those which are supposed to originate in the mind, or which are more immediately applied to it. Such are, the long endurance of grief; ardent and ungratified desires; religious terror; the disappointment of pride; sudden fright; fits of anger; prosperity humbled by misfortunes:[15] in short, the frequent and uncurbed indulgence of any passion or emotion, and any sudden or violent affection of the mind.

There are, doubtless, many other causes of both classes, which may tend to produce this disease. Those which have been stated, are such as I am most familiar with; or, to speak more accurately, such are the circumstances most generally found to have preceded this affection.

It is an old opinion, and continues still to prevail, that maniacs are influenced by the changes of the moon. In the fourth chapter of St. Matthew's Gospel, verse 24, we find the word "Σεληνιαξομένους" which is rendered in the English version, "those which were lunatic." Notwithstanding the notion of being moon-struck might prevail among the ignorant people of Galilee, yet Hippocrates, a philosopher, and correct observer of natural phænomena, does not appear to have placed any faith in this planetary influence. Although the Romans were infected with this popular tradition, as may be seen in the following passage of the Art of Poetry,

"Ut mala quem scabies aut morbus regius urget,
Aut fanaticus error, et iracunda Diana
Vesanum tetigisse timent fugiuntque poetam,
Qui sapiunt:"—

yet Celsus did not consider the operation of the moon on the human intellect sufficiently well founded to admit it into his medical work. Not a word on this subject is mentioned in the eighteenth chapter of his third book, which particularly treats of Insanity, "*De tribus insaniæ generibus*;" it is true that, in the fourth chapter of the first book, which speaks "*De his quibus caput infirmum est*," he says "Cui caput infirmum est, is si bene concoxit, leniter perfricare id mane manibus suis debet; nunquam id, si fieri potest, veste velare; aut ad cutem tondere: utileque lunam vitare, maximeque ante ipsum lunæ solisque concursum." By the *infirmum caput*, Celsus does not mean madness, as may be clearly seen by perusing the chapter: the weakness of intellect, which frequently continues after fever, or other violent diseases, is evidently his meaning; but Dr. Cox has quoted the above passage, to prove that Celsus was impressed with the truth of this vulgar opinion. He says, "This idea of lunar influence, in *maniacal complaints*, was handed down to us by our medical forefathers, and is still very generally adopted."

It is most probable that this idea of planetary regency, however it might have arisen, or to whatever extent it may have been credited, received in the Arabian school, the stamp by which its currency has been subsequently maintained. For the revival and dispersion of ancient medical knowledge, we are confessedly under considerable obligations to the Arabians;[16] and more especially for the incorporation of astrology, magic and alchymy, with medicine.

Popular superstitions and national proverbs, are seldom without some foundation; and with respect to the present, it may be observed, that if it were not in some degree rooted in fact, and trained up by observation, it would become difficult to ascertain how such an opinion came to be adopted; and this investigation is rendered still more important from the consideration, that the existing law in this country, respecting insane persons, has been established on the supposed prevalence of this lunar regulation. A commission is issued, de *lunatico* inquirendo, and the commissioners sitting for that purpose, are particular in their enquiries, whether the patient enjoys lucid intervals. The term *lucid interval* has been properly connected with the word *lunacy*; for, if the patient, as they supposed, became insane at particular changes of the moon, the inference was natural, that in the intervening spaces of time he would become rational.

It is more than probable, that the origin of this supposition of the lunar influence may be traced to the following circumstances. The period of the return of the moon, and of regular menstruation in women, is four weeks; and the terms which designate them, have been imposed from the period of time in which both are compleated. Insanity and epilepsy are often connected with menstruation, and suffer an exacerbation of their paroxysms at the period when this discharge happens, or ought to take place. If, therefore, the period of menstruation in an insane woman should occur at the full of the moon, and her mind should then be more violently disturbed, the recurrence of the same state may be naturally expected at the next full moon. This is a necessary coincidence, and should be discriminated from effect. But such has been the prevalence of this opinion, that when patients have been brought to Bethlem hospital, especially those from the country, their friends have generally stated them to be worse at some particular change of the moon, and of the necessity they were under, at those times, to have recourse to a severer coercion. Indeed, I have understood from some of these *lunatics*, who have recovered, that the overseer or master of the work-house himself has frequently been so much under the dominion of this planet, and keeping steadily in mind the old maxim, *venienti occurrite morbo*, that, without waiting for any display of increased turbulence on the part of the patient, he has bound, chained, flogged, and deprived these miserable people of food, according as he discovered the moon's age by the almanack.

To ascertain how far this opinion was founded in fact, I kept, during more than two years, an exact register, but without finding, in any instance, that the aberrations of the human intellect corresponded with, or were influenced by, the vicissitudes of this luminary.

As insane persons, especially those in a furious state, are but little disposed to sleep, even under the most favourable circumstances, they will be still less so, when the moon shines brightly into their apartments.

It has also been considered, that intellectual labour frequently becomes a cause of insanity; that those, who are in the habit of exercising the faculty of thought, for the perfection and preservation of the reason of others, are thereby in danger of losing their own. We hear much of this, from those who have copiously treated of this disease, without the toil of practical remark; whose heads become bewildered by the gentlest exercise, and to whom the recreation of thinking becomes the exciting cause of stupidity or delirium. These persons enumerate, among the exciting causes of delirium, "Too great, or too long continued exertion of the mental faculties, as in the delirium which often succeeds long continued and abstract calculation; and the deliria to which men of genius are peculiarly subject."

The mind of every man is capable of a definite quantity of exertion to good effect; all endeavours, beyond that point, are impotent and perplexing. The attention is capable of being fixed to a certain extent, and, when that begins to deviate, all continuance is time lost. It is certain that, by habit, this power may be much increased; and, by frequent exercise, that, which at first excited fatigue, may be continued with facility and pleasure. What species of delirium is that, which succeeds long continued and abstract calculation? Newton lived to the age of 85 years, Leibnitz to 70, and Euler to a more advanced period, yet their several biographers have neglected to inform us, that their studies were checquered with delirious fermentations. The mathematicians of the present day (and there are many of distinguished eminence) would conceive it no compliment to suppose that they retired from their labours with addled brains, and that writers of books on insanity should impute to them miseries which they never experienced.

It is curious to remark, in looking over a biographical chart, that mathematicians and natural philosophers have in general attained a considerable age; so that long continued and abstract calculation, or correct thinking upon any subject does not appear, with all these delirious visitations, to shorten the duration of human life. What is meant by the deliria, to which men of genius are peculiarly subject, I am unable, from a want of sufficient genius and delirium, to comprehend.

It is well understood, that a want of rational employment is a very successful mode of courting delirium; that an indulgence in those reveries which keep the imagination on the wing, and imprison the understanding, is likely to promote it: and it must be owned, that the same effect has often been produced, where vanity or ambition has urged minds, puny by nature, and undrilled in intellectual exercises, to attempt to grasp that which they were unable to embrace. This may be illustrated by the following case.

A young gentleman of slender capacity, and very moderate education, at the age of nineteen, was placed in a merchant's counting house, where he continued for two years diligently, though slowly, to perform the duties of the office. Coming at this time into the possession of considerable property, and perhaps, aware of the uncultivated state of his own mind, he very laudably determined to improve it. He frequented the society of persons esteemed learned and eminent in their different professions, and became much delighted with their conversation; but at the same time sensible that he was unable to contribute to the discourse. He resolved to become a severe student, and for this purpose purchased an immense quantity of books on most subjects of literature and science. History commenced the career of his enquiries: Rollin, Gibbon, Hume and Robertson were anxiously and rapidly perused; but he never paused to consider, or to connect dates and circumstances, so that these excellent authors, after he had waded through them, left scarcely an impression on his mind. Chemistry next engaged his attention, and on this subject, he pored over many volumes with little advantage: the terms proved a source of embarrassment, and he made no experiments. In a hasty succession, the ancient languages, antiquities, etymology, agriculture, and moral philosophy, occupied his mind. About eight hours were daily devoted to reading. Somewhat more than two years were consumed in this employment, which had distracted his mind, without conferring any positive knowledge.

His friends and acquaintances now began to perceive a considerable alteration in his temper; though naturally diffident, he had assumed a high degree of literary importance, and plumed himself on the extent of his learning. Before this excessive, but ill-directed application, he was a strict relator of the truth, but he now found a convenience in supplying by fancy, that, which the indigence of his memory was unable to afford. Shortly he began to complain that he could not sleep, and that the long night was passed in shifting from side to side.

"Lasso, ch'n van te chiamo, et queste oscure,
Et gelide ombre in van lusingo: o piume

D'asprezza colme: o notti acerbe, et dure."
Gio: Della Casa.

Fever succeeded, accompanied with delirium in the evening. By quietness, and the ordinary remedies, these symptoms were removed; but he was left in a state of extreme weakness. As he recovered from this, his habits became materially altered: he would continue to lie in bed for several days, after which, he would suddenly rise and walk a number of miles. Personal cleanliness, and dress were entirely neglected: sometimes he would fast for two or three days, and then eat voraciously. Afterwards he became suspicious that poison had been mixed with his food. It was found necessary to confine him, from having attempted to castrate himself: this he afterwards effected in a very complete manner, and continues a maniac to the present time.

Few persons, I believe, will be disposed to consider the above case, as an instance of insanity succeeding to a laborious exercise of the intellectual faculties. It is true, he was busied with books: but this occupation could not have strained his mind, for he appears neither to have comprehended, nor retained any of the objects of his pursuit.

Hereditary Disposition.

"Ut male posuimus initia sic cetera sequuntur."—*Cicero.*

"Whatever was in the womb imperfect, as to her proper work, comes very rarely, or never at all, to perfection afterwards."—*Harrington's Works, p.* 177.

Considerable diversity of opinion has prevailed, whether insanity be hereditary or not; and much has been said on both sides of this question. Great ingenuity has been exerted to prove that this disease is accidental, or that there are sufficient causes to account for its occurrence, without supposing it one of those calamities that *"flesh is heir to."* It has been argued, that, if the disease were hereditary, it ought uniformly to be so, and that the offspring of a mad parent should necessarily become insane.

All theories and reasonings appear to be good for as much as they prove; and if the term *hereditary* be employed with a degree of strictness, so as to denote certain and infallible transmission, such inevitable descent cannot be defended. Several instances have come under my observation where the children of an insane parent have not hitherto been affected with madness, and some have died early in life, without having experienced any derangement of mind. More time is therefore required.

All observations concur in acknowledging that there are many circumstances in which children resemble their parents. It is very common to see them resemble one of their parents in countenance, and when there are several children, some shall bear the likeness of the father and others of the mother. Children often possess the make and fashion of the body, peculiar to one or other of their parents, together with their gait and voice; but that which has surprized me most is the resemblance of the hand-writing. If a parent had taught his son to write, it might be expected that a considerable similarity would be detected; but in general the fact appears to be otherwise, for it seldom happens that the scholars, though constantly imitating the copy of the master, write at all like him, or like each other. In a few instances I have noticed a correct resemblance between the hand-writing of the father and son, where the former died before the latter had been taught the use of the pen, and who probably never saw the hand-writing of his father. The transmission of personal deformities is equally curious. I am acquainted with a person in this town, whose middle and ring finger are united, and act as one; all the children of this man carry the same defect. A toenail, particularly twisted, has been traced through three generations, on the same foot and toe. Abundant instances might be adduced on this subject; there is scarcely a family which cannot produce something in confirmation; and if to these circumstances in the human species, were to be added the experiments which have been made on the breeding of cattle, perhaps little doubt would remain.

The reasoners against the transmission of madness urge, that, if the contrary were true, we should by this time have detected the rule or law by which nature acts, and that we should have been able to determine,—First, whether the disorder descended to the male or female children accordingly as the father or mother was affected.—Secondly, which of the parents is most capable of transmitting the disease?—Thirdly, what alternations in the succession take place, does it shift from the male to the female line, and, does it miss a generation, and afterwards return?

These, and a multitude of other queries, might be proposed; I believe much faster than they could be answered. Nature appears to delight in producing new varieties, perhaps less in man than in other animals, and still less in the animal than in the vegetable kingdom. Before these subtile reasoners expect, from those who maintain that madness generally descends from the parent to the offspring, a developement of the laws by which Nature acts, it would be convenient first to settle whether in this matter she be under the dominion of any law whatever.

The investigation of the hereditary tendency of madness is an object of the utmost importance, both in a legal and moral point of view. Parents and guardians, in the disposal, or direction of the choice of their children in marriage, should be informed, that an alliance with a family, where insanity has prevailed, ought to be prohibited.

Having directed some attention to enquiries of this nature, I am enabled truly to state, that, where one of the parents have been insane, it is more than probable that the offsprings will be similarly affected.

Madness has many colours, and colours have many hues; actual madness is a severe calamity, yet experience has pointed out the treatment, and the law has permitted the imposition of the necessary restraint: but it very frequently occurs that the descendants from an insane stock, although they do not exhibit the broad features of madness, shall yet discover propensities, equally disqualifying for the purposes of life, and destructive of social happiness.

The slighter shades of this disease include eccentricity, low spirits, and oftentimes a fatal tendency to immoral habits, notwithstanding the inculcation of the most correct precepts, and the force of virtuous example.

In illustration of the fact, that the offsprings of insane persons are, *ceteris paribus*, more liable to be affected with madness than those whose parents have been of sound minds; it was my intention to have constructed a table, whereon might be seen the probably direct course of this disease, and also its collateral bearings: but difficulties have arisen. It appeared, on consideration, improper to attempt precision with that which was variable, and as yet unsettled; I have therefore been content to select a few histories from my book of notes, and to exhibit them in the rude state in which they were set down.

1st.—R. G. His grandfather was mad, but there was no insanity in his grandmother's family. His father was occasionally melancholic, and once had a raving paroxysm. His mother's family was sane. His father's brother died insane. R. G. has a brother and five sisters; his brother has been confined in St. Luke's, and is occasionally in a low spirited state. All his sisters have been insane; with the three youngest the disease came on after delivery.

2d.—M. M. Her grandmother was insane and destroyed herself. Her father was mad for many years, but after the birth of all his children. M. M. has two brothers and a sister; both her brothers have been insane; the sister has never been so affected, but was a person of loose character. The insanity of M. M. was connected with her menstruation; after its cessation she recovered, although she had been confined more than sixteen years.

3d.—M. H. Her father had been several times insane; her mother was likewise so affected a few months before her death. Afterwards her father married a woman perfectly sane, by whom he had three children, two female and a male; both the females are melancholic, the male was a vicious character, and has been transported. M. H. has had ten children, three have died with convulsions, the eldest, a girl, is epileptic.

4th.—T. B. His mother became insane soon after being delivered of him, and at intervals has continued so ever since. He has a brother who became furiously mad at the age of twenty, and afterwards recovered. T. B.'s disorder came on at the age of twenty-six.

5th.—S. F. Her father's mother was insane, and confined in the hospital. Her father never discovered any symptoms of insanity, and her mother was perfectly sane. Her only sister (she had no brothers) was mad about five years ago, and recovered. S. F. has been twice in the hospital.

6th.—P. W. After the best enquiries it does not appear that her father or mother ever experienced any attack of madness or melancholy. P. W.'s disorder commenced shortly after the delivery of a child. She has three sisters, the eldest has never been married, and has hitherto continued of sound mind. The two younger have been mothers, and in both insanity has supervened on childbearing.

7th.—J. A. H. His father's father was insane, and his father was also disordered, and destroyed himself. His mother was of sound mind. J. A. H. became insane at the age of twenty-three. He has two sisters, the elder has once been confined for insanity, the younger is of weak intellects, nearly approaching to ideotism.

8th.—M. D. Her mother was insane and died so. M. D. continued of sane mind until she had attained the age of fifty-seven, when she became furiously maniacal; her only daughter, eighteen years of age, was attacked with mania during the time her mother was confined.

9th.—G. F. His mother was melancholic during the time she was pregnant with him, and never afterwards completely recovered. She had five children previously to this melancholic attack, who have hitherto continued of sound mind. She bore another son after G. F. who is extremely flighty and unmanageable. G. F. was attacked with madness at the age of nineteen, and died apoplectic, from the violence and continued fury of his disorder.

10th.—M. T. Her mother was of sound mind. Her father was in a melancholic state for two years, before she was born, but this was afterwards dissipated by active employment. M. T.

has two brothers, younger than herself, who have been attacked with insanity, neither of whom have recovered. She has two sisters, some years older than herself, these have never been deranged. M. T. has had nine children. The three first have been melancholic. The youngest, at the age of five years, used to imagine she saw persons in the room covered with blood, and other horrible objects, she afterwards became epileptic and died. The youngest of her three first children has been married and had three children, one of whom is afflicted with chorea Sancti Viti, and another is nearly an ideot.

Of the causes termed moral, the greatest number may, perhaps, be traced to the errors of education, which often plant in the youthful mind those seeds of madness which the slightest circumstances readily awaken into growth.

It should be as much the object of the teachers of youth, to subjugate the passions, as to discipline the intellect. The tender mind should be prepared to expect the natural and certain effects of causes: its propensity to indulge an avaricious thirst for that which is unattainable, should be quenched: nor should it be suffered to acquire a fixed and invincible attachment to that which is fleeting and perishable.

Of the more immediate, or, as it is generally termed, the proximate cause of this disease, I profess to know nothing. Whenever the functions of the brain shall be fully understood, and the use of its different parts ascertained, we may then be enabled to judge, how far disease, attacking any of these parts, may increase, diminish, or otherwise alter its functions. But this is a degree of knowledge, which we are not likely soon to attain. It seems, however, not improbable, that the only source, from whence the most copious and certain information can be drawn, is a strict attention to the particular appearances which morbid states of this organ may present.

From the preceding dissections of insane persons, it may be inferred, that madness has always been connected with disease of the brain and of its membranes. Having no particular theory to build up, they have been related purely for the advancement of science and of truth.

It may be a matter, affording much diversity of opinion, whether these morbid appearances of the brain be the cause or the effect of madness: it may be observed that they have been found in all states of the disease. When the brain has been injured from external violence, its functions have been generally impaired, if inflammation of its substance, or more delicate membranes has ensued. The same appearances have for the most part been detected, when patients have died of phrenitis, or in the delirium of fever: in these instances, the derangement of the intellectual functions appears evidently to have been caused by the inflammation. If in mania the same appearances be found, there will be no necessity of calling in the aid of other causes, to account for the effect: indeed, it would be difficult to discover them.

Those who entertain an opposite opinion are obliged to suppose, *a disease of the mind.* Such a morbid affection, from the limited nature of my powers, perhaps I have never been able to conceive. Possessing, however, little knowledge of metaphysical controversy, I shall only offer a few remarks upon this part of the subject, and beg pardon for having at all touched it.

Perhaps it is not more difficult to suppose, that matter, peculiarly arranged, may *think,*[17] than to conceive the union of an immaterial being with a corporeal substance. It is questioning the infinite wisdom and power of the Deity to say, that he does not, or cannot, arrange matter so that it shall think. When we find insanity, as far as has been hitherto observed, uniformly accompanied with disease of the brain, is it not more just to conclude, that such organic affection has produced this incorrect association of ideas, than that a being, which is immaterial, incorruptible, and immortal, should be subject to the gross and subordinate changes which matter necessarily undergoes?

But let us imagine *a disease of ideas*. In what manner are we to effect a cure? To this subtle spirit the doctor can apply no medicines. Though so refined as to elude the force of material remedies, some may however think that it may be reasoned with. The good effects which have resulted from exhibiting logic as a remedy for madness, must be sufficiently known to every one who has conversed with insane persons, and must be considered as time very judiciously employed: speaking more gravely, it will readily be acknowledged, by persons acquainted with this disease, that, if insanity be a disease of ideas, we can possess no corporeal remedies for it: and that an endeavour to convince madmen of their errors, by reasoning, is folly in those who attempt it, since there is always in madness the firmest conviction of the truth of what is false, and which the clearest and most circumstantial evidence cannot remove.

CHAP. VI.

ON THE PROBABLE EVENT OF THE DISEASE.

THE prediction of the event, in cases of insanity, must be the result of accurate and extensive experience; and even then it will probably be a matter of very great uncertainty. The practitioner can only be led to suppose, that patients, of a particular description, will recover, from knowing that, under the same circumstances, a certain number have been actually restored to sanity of intellect.

The practice of an individual, however active and industrious he may be, is insufficient to accumulate a stock of facts, necessary to form the ground of a regular and correct prognosis: it is therefore to be wished, that those, who exclusively confine themselves to this department of the profession, would occasionally communicate to the world the result of their observations.

Physicians, attending generally to diseases, have not been reserved, in imparting to the public the amount of their labours and success: but, with regard to this disorder, those, who have devoted their whole attention to its treatment, have either been negligent, or cautious of giving information respecting it. Whenever the powers of the mind are concentrated to one object, we may naturally expect a more rapid progress in the attainment of knowledge: we have therefore only to lament the want of observations upon this subject, and endeavour to repair it.

The records of Bethlem Hospital have afforded me some satisfactory information, though far from the whole of what I wished to obtain. From them, and my own observations, the prognosis of this disease is, with great diffidence, submitted to the reader.

In our own climate, women are more frequently afflicted with insanity than men. Several persons, who superintend private mad-houses, have assured me, that the number of females brought in annually, considerably exceeds that of the males. From the year 1748 to 1794, comprizing a period of forty-six years, there have been admitted into Bethlem Hospital, 4832 women, and 4042 men.

The natural processes, which women undergo, of menstruation, parturition, and of preparing nutriment for the infant, together with the diseases, to which they are subject at these periods, and which are frequently remote causes of insanity, may, perhaps, serve to explain their greater disposition to this malady. As to the proportion in which they recover, compared with males, it may be stated, that of 4832 women affected, 1402 were discharged cured; and that, of the 4042 men, 1155 recovered. It is proper here to mention, that, in general, we know but little of what becomes of those who are discharged; a certain number of those cured, occasionally relapse, and some of those, who are discharged uncured, afterwards recover: perhaps in the majority of instances where they relapse, they are sent back to Bethlem. To give some idea of the number, so re-admitted, it may be mentioned, that, during the last two years,[18] there have been admitted 389 patients, 53 of whom had at some former time been in the house. There are so many circumstances, which, supposing they did relapse, might prevent them from returning, that it can only be stated with certainty, that within twelve months, the time allowed as a trial of cure, so many have been discharged perfectly well.

To shew how frequently insanity supervenes on parturition, it may be remarked, that from the year 1784 to 1794 inclusive, 80 patients have been admitted, whose disorder shortly followed the puerperal state. Women affected from this cause, recover in a larger proportion than patients of any other description of the same age. Of these 80, 50 have perfectly recovered. The first symptoms of the approach of this disease after delivery, are want of sleep; the countenance becomes flushed; a constrictive pain is often felt in the head; the eyes assume a morbid lustre, and wildly glance at objects in rapid succession; the milk is afterwards secreted in less quantity; and when the mind becomes more violently disordered, it is totally suppressed. Where the disease is hereditary, parturition very frequently becomes an exciting cause.

From whatever cause this disease may be produced in women, it is considered as very unfavourable to recovery, if they should be worse at the period of menstruation, or have their catamenia in very small or immoderate quantities.

A few cases have occurred where the disease, being connected with menstruation, and having continued many years, has completely disappeared on the cessation of the uterine discharge.

At the first attack of this disease, and for some months afterwards, during its continuance, females most commonly labour under amenorrhœa. The natural and healthy return of this discharge generally precedes convalescence.

From the following statement it will be seen, that insane persons recover in proportion to their youth, and that as they advance in years, the disease is less frequently cured. It comprizes a period of about ten years, viz. from 1784 to 1794. In the first column the age is noticed; in the second, the number of patients admitted; the third contains the number cured; the fourth, those who were discharged not cured.

Age between	Number admitted.	Number discharged cured.	Number discharged uncured.
10 and 20	113	78	35
20 and 30	488	200	288
30 and 40	527	180	347
40 and 50	362	87	275
50 and 60	143	25	118
60 and 70	31	4	27
Total	1664	Total 574	Total 1090

From this table it will be seen, that when the disease attacks persons advanced in life, the prospect of recovery is but small.

I am led to conclude, from the very rare instances of complete cure, or durable amendment, among the class of patients deemed incurable, as well as from the infrequent recovery of those who have been admitted, after the disorder has been of more than twelve months standing, that the chance of cure is less, in proportion to the length of time which the disorder shall have continued.

Although patients, who have been affected with insanity more than a year, are not admissible into the hospital, to continue there for the usual time of trial for cure, namely, a twelvemonth, yet, at the discretion of the committee, they may be received into it, from Lady-day to Michaelmas, at which latter period they are removed. In the course of the last twenty years seventy-eight patients of this description have been received, of whom only one has been discharged cured: this patient, who was a woman, has since relapsed twice, and was ultimately sent from the hospital uncured.

When the reader contrasts the preceding statement with the account recorded in the report of the Committee, appointed to examine the Physicians who have attended His Majesty, &c. he will either be inclined to deplore the unskilfulness or mismanagement which has prevailed among those medical persons who have directed the treatment of mania in the largest public institution in this kingdom, of its kind, compared with the success which has attended the private practice of an individual; *or to require some other evidence, than the bare assertion of the man pretending to have performed such cures.*[19]

It was deposed by that reverend and celebrated physician, that of patients placed under his care, within three months after the attack of the disease, nine out of ten had recovered;[20] and also that the age was of no signification, unless the patient had been afflicted before with the same malady.[21]

How little soever I might be disposed to doubt such a bold, unprecedented, and marvellous account, yet, I must acknowledge, that my mind would have been much more satisfied, as to the truth of that assertion, had it been plausibly made out, or had the circumstances been otherwise than feebly recollected by that very successful practitioner. Medicine has generally been esteemed a progressive science, in which its professors have confessed themselves indebted to great preparatory study and long subsequent experience for the knowledge they have acquired; but, in the case to which we are now alluding, the outset of the Doctor's practice was marked with such splendid success, that time and observation have been unable to increase it.

This astonishing number of cures has been effected by the vigorous agency of remedies, which others have not hitherto been so fortunate as to discover; by remedies, which, when remote causes have been operating for twenty-seven years, such as weighty business, severe exercise, too great abstemiousness and little rest, are possessed of adequate power directly to *meet and counteract* such causes.[22]

It will be seen by the preceding table, that a greater number of patients have been admitted, between the age of 30 and 40, than during any other equal period of life. The same fact also obtains in France, as may be seen from the statement of Dr. Pinel, (*Traité Medico-Philosophique sur la Manie*, *p.* 109,) and which, from its agreement with that of Bethlem Hospital, is here introduced to the notice of the reader.

Maniacal Patients admitted into the Bicêtre, in the Years	AGE BETWEEN						Total
	15 & 20	20 & 30	30 & 40	40 & 50	50 & 60	60 & 70	
1784	5	33	31	24	11	6	110
1785	4	39	49	25	14	3	134
1786	4	31	40	32	15	5	127
1787	12	39	41	26	17	7	142
1788	9	43	53	21	18	7	151
1789	6	38	39	33	14	2	132
1790	6	28	34	19	9	7	103
1791	9	26	32	16	7	3	93
1792	6	26	33	18	12	3	98
1793	1	13	13	7	4	2	40
1794	3	23	15	15	9	6	71

There may be some reasons assigned for the increased proportion of insane persons at this age. Although I have made no exact calculation, yet from a great number of cases, it appears to be the time when the hereditary disposition is most frequently called into action; or, to speak more plainly, it is that stage of life, when persons, whose families have been insane, are most liable to become mad. If it can be made to appear, that at this period persons are more subject to be acted upon by the remote causes of the disease, or that a greater number of such causes are then applied, we may be able satisfactorily to explain it.

At this age people are generally established in their different occupations, are married, and have families; their habits are more strongly formed, and the interruptions of them are consequently attended with greater anxiety and regret. Under these circumstances, they feel the misfortunes of life more exquisitely. Adversity does not depress the individual for himself alone, but as involving his partner and his offspring in wretchedness and ruin. In youth we feel desirous only of present good; at the middle age, we become more provident and anxious for the future; the mind assumes a serious character; and religion, as it is justly or improperly impressed, imparts comfort, or excites apprehension and terror.

By misfortunes the habit of intoxication is readily formed. Those who in their youth have shaken off calamity as a slight incumbrance, at the middle age feel it corrode and penetrate; and when fermented liquors have once dispelled the gloom of despondency, and taught the mind to provoke a temporary assemblage of cheerful scenes, or to despise the terror of impending misery, it is natural to recur to the same, though destructive cause, to re-produce the effect.

Patients, who are in a furious state, recover in a larger proportion than those who are depressed and melancholic. An hundred violent, and the same number of melancholic cases were selected: of the former, sixty-two were discharged well; of the latter, only twenty-seven: subsequent experience has confirmed this fact. The same investigation, on the same number of persons has been twice instituted, and with results little varying from the originally stated proportions. When the furious state is succeeded by melancholy, and after this shall have continued a short time, the violent paroxysm returns, the chance of recovery is very slight. Indeed, whenever these states of the disease frequently change, such alteration may be considered as very unfavourable.

After a raving paroxysm of considerable duration, it is a hopeful symptom, if the patient become dull, and in a stupid state; inclined to sleep much, and feeling a desire of quietude. This appears to be the natural effect of that exhaustion, and, if the language be allowable, of that expenditure of the sensorial energy, which the continued blaze of furious madness would necessarily consume. When they gradually recover from this state there is a prospect that the cure will be permanent.

In forming a prognosis of this disease, it is highly important to establish a distinction between derangement and decline of intellect: the former may frequently be remedied; the latter admits of no assistance from our art. Where insanity commences with a loss of mental faculty, and gradually proceeds with increasing imbecility, the case may be considered hopeless.

When the disorder has been induced from remote physical causes, the proportion of those who recover is considerably greater, than where it has arisen from causes of a moral nature. In those instances where insanity has been produced by a train of unavoidable misfortunes, as where the father of a large family, with the most laborious exertions, ineffectually struggles to maintain it, the number who recover is very small indeed.

Paralytic affections are a much more frequent cause of insanity than has been commonly supposed, and they are also a very common effect of madness; more maniacs die of hemiplegia and apoplexy than from any other disease. In those affected from this cause, we are, on enquiry, enabled to trace a sudden affection, or fit, to have preceded the disease. These patients usually bear marks of such affection, independently of their insanity: the speech is impeded, and the mouth drawn aside; an arm, or leg, is more or less deprived of its capability of being moved by the will: and in most of them the memory is particularly impaired. Persons thus disordered are in general not at all sensible of being so affected. When so feeble, as scarcely to be able to stand, they commonly say that they feel perfectly strong, and capable of great exertions. However pitiable these objects may be to the feeling spectator, yet it is fortunate for the condition of the sufferer, that his pride and pretensions are usually exalted in proportion to the degradation of the calamity which afflicts him. None of these patients have received any benefit in the hospital; and from the enquiries I have been able to make at the private mad-houses, where they have been afterwards confined, it has appeared, that they have either died suddenly, from apoplexy, or have had repeated fits, from the effects of which they have sunk into a stupid state, and gradually dwindled away.

The paralytic require to be kept warm, and to be allowed a more nutritious diet and cheering beverage than insane patients of any other description. In the winter months they suffer extremely, and ought to be treated as hot-house plants.

The fare of the workhouse is ungenial to this wretched state of existence, and therefore they seldom long continue a burden to the parish.

When insanity supervenes on epilepsy, or where the latter disease is induced by insanity, a cure is very seldom effected. In two instances I have known madness alternate with epilepsy: one, a man about forty-eight years of age, was a pauper in the Cripplegate workhouse, where he had been kept about three years on account of his epileptic fits, but, becoming insane, was admitted into Bethlem Hospital, therein he continued a year, without being at all benefited; during that time he had no epileptic fit. Being returned to the workhouse, he there recovered his senses in a few months, when his epileptic attacks returned, and continued with their usual frequency. About two years afterwards he was re-admitted into the hospital, his insanity having recurred, and continued there another year without experiencing any attack of epilepsy. The other was a young woman, who had been epileptic for many years until she became insane, when she lost her epileptic fits; these, however, were said to have returned in a short time after she had recovered from her insanity.

All authors who have treated this subject appear to agree respecting the difficulty of curing religious madness. The infrequent recoveries in this species of insanity, have caused thinking persons to suppose, that this disorder is little under the dominion of the medical practitioner; and, that restoration to reason in all cases is more the effect of accident, or of circumstances not "dreamt of in our philosophy," than the result of observation, skill, and experience. The idea that Religion; that which fastens us to the duties of this life; that which expounds the laws of God and of his creation to the ignorant; that which administers consolation to the afflicted;

that which regulates man's conduct towards his fellow creatures, to exercise charity among them, and, from such benevolence, to purchase happiness to himself: to believe, that the cultivation of such exalted sentiments would decoy a human being into madness, is a foolish and impious supposition.

"Thou, fair Religion, wast design'd,
Duteous daughter of the skies,
To warm and chear the human mind,
To make men happy, good, and wise;
To point, where sits in love array'd,
Attentive to each suppliant call,
The God of universal aid,
The God, the Father of us all.

"First shewn by Thee, thus glow'd the gracious scene,
'Til Superstition, fiend of woe,
Bad doubts to rise and tears to flow,
And spread deep shades our view and heaven between."
Penrose.

It is therefore sinful to accuse Religion, which preserves the dignity and integrity of our intellectual faculty, with being the cause of its derangement. The mind becomes refreshed and corroborated by a fair and active exercise of its powers directed to proper objects; but when an anxious curiosity leads us to unveil that which must ever be shrouded from our view, the despair, which always attends those impotent researches, will necessarily reduce us to the most calamitous state.

Instituting a generous and tolerant survey of religious opinions, we see nothing in the solemn pomp of catholic worship which could disorganize the mind; as human beings, they have employed human art to render the impression more vivid and durable. The decorous piety, and exemplary life of the quaker has signally exempted him from this most severe of human infirmities. The established church of this country, of which I am an unworthy member, will delude no one, by its terrors, to the brink of fatuity: the solid wisdom, rational exposition, and pure charity, which flow through the works of Taylor, Barrow, Secker, and Tillotson, will inspire their readers with a manly confidence: the most enlightened of our species will advance in wisdom and in happiness from their perusal; and the simplicity and truth of their comments will be evident to those of less cultivated understanding. The pastors of this church are all men of liberal education, and many have attained the highest literary character; they are therefore eminently qualified to afford instruction. But what can be expected, when the most ignorant of our race attempt to inform the multitude; when the dregs of society shall assume the garb of sanctity and the holy office; and pretend to point out a privy path to heaven, or cozen their feeble followers into the belief that they possess a picklock for its gates? The difficulty of curing this species of madness will be readily explained from the consideration, that the whole of their doctrine is a base system of delusion, rivetted on the mind by terror and despair; and there is also good reason to suppose, that they frequently contrive, by the grace of cordials, to fix the waverings of belief, and thus endeavour to dispel the gloom and dejection which these hallucinations infallibly excite.

Although the faction of faith will owe me no kindness for the disclosure of these opinions, yet it would be ungrateful were I to shrink from the avowal of my obligations to methodism[23] for the supply of those numerous cases which has constituted my experience of this wretched calamity.

When the natural small-pox attacks insane persons it most commonly proves fatal. I was induced to draw this conclusion from consulting the records of Bethlem, where I found that few of those who had been sent to the Small-pox Hospital recovered; but subsequent experience has enabled me to point out this distinction: that those who have been in a furious state have generally experienced a fatal termination, and that those who recovered had the small-pox when they were in a state of convalescence from their insanity.

When patients, during their convalescence, become more corpulent than they were before, it is a favourable symptom; and, as far as I have remarked, such persons have very seldom relapsed. But it should also be observed, that many, who become stupid, and in a state, verging on ideotism, are very much disposed to obesity: these cases are not to be remedied.

In proportion as insanity has assumed a systematic character, it become more difficult of cure. It ought to be noticed, that this state of methodical madness implies, that the disease has been of some continuance; and, to use a figurative expression, has been more extensively rooted in the mind. Every occurrence is blended with the ruling persuasion, and the delusion becomes daily corroborated. As

—————"Trifles, light as air,
Are to the jealous, confirmations strong
As proofs of holy writ;"

so in madness, circumstances wholly unconnected readily support the favourite system, and persons the most disinterested are supposed to form a part of the conspiracy.

CHAP. VII.

MANAGEMENT.

OUR own countrymen have acquired the credit of managing insane people with superior address; but it does not appear that we have arrogated to ourselves any such invidious pre-eminence. Foreigners, who have visited the public or private institutions of this country, may, perhaps, in their relations, have magnified our skill in the treatment of this disease: compared with a great part of the north of Europe, which I have visited, we certainly excel.

Whether it be that we have more mad persons in England than in other countries, and thereby have derived a greater experience of this calamity; or, whether the greater number of receptacles we possess for the insane, and the emoluments which have resulted from this species of farming, have led persons to speculate more particularly on the nature and treatment of this affection, may be difficult to determine. Dr. Pinel[24] allows the reputation we have acquired; but, with a laudable curiosity, is desirous to understand how we became possessed of it.

"Is it," he says, "from a peculiar national pride, and to display their superiority over other nations, that the English boast of their ability in curing madness by moral remedies; and at the same time conceal the cunning of this art with an impenetrable veil? or, on the contrary, may not that which we attribute to a subtile policy, be merely the effect of circumstances? and, is it not necessary to distinguish the steps of the English empirics from the methods of treatment adopted in their public hospitals?

"Whatever solution may be given to these questions, yet, after fifteen years diligent enquiry, in order to ascertain some of the leading features of this method, from the reports of travellers; the accounts published of such establishments; the notices concerning their public and private receptacles, which are to be found in the different journals, or in the works of their medical writers, I can affirm, that I have never been able to discover any development of this English secret for the treatment of insanity, though all concur in the ability of their management. Speaking of Dr. Willis,[25] it is said, that sweetness and affability seem to dwell upon his countenance; but its character changes the moment he looks on a patient: the whole of his features suddenly assume a different aspect, which enforces respect and attention from the insane. His penetrating eye appears to search into their hearts, and arrest their thoughts as they arise. Thus he establishes a dominion, which is afterwards employed as a principal agent of cure. But, where is the elucidation of these general principles to be sought; and, in what manner are they to be applied according to the character, varieties, and intensity of madness? Is the work of Dr. Arnold otherwise remarkable than as a burdensome compilation, or a multiplication of scholastic divisions, more calculated to retard than advance the progress of Science? Does Dr. Harpur, who announces in his preface, that he has quitted the beaten track, fulfil his promise in the course of his work? and is his section on mental indications any thing but a prolix commentary on the doctrines of the ancients? The adventurous spirit of Dr. Crichton, may justly excite admiration, who has published two volumes on maniacal and melancholic affections, merely on the authority of some observations drained from a German Journal; together with ingenious dissertations on the doctrines of modern physiologists, and a view of the moral and physical effects of the human passions. Finally, can a mere advertisement of Dr. Fowler's establishment for the insane in Scotland, throw any light on the particular management of such persons, although it profess the purest and most dignified humanity, successfully operating on the moral treatment of madness?"

Dr. Pinel is deserving of considerable credit for directing the attention of medical men to this very important point of the moral management of the insane. I have also heard much of this fascinating power which the mad doctor is said to possess over the wayward lunatic; but, from all I have observed amongst the eminent practitioners of the present day, who exercise this department of the profession, I am led to suspect, that, although this influence may have been formerly possessed, and even to the extent attributed to the late reverend doctor, it ought now to be lamented among the *artes deperditæ*. Could the attention of lunatics be fixed, and could they be reduced to obedience, by

"Strong impression and strange powers which lie
Within the magic circle of the eye,"

all other kinds of restraint would be superfluous and unnecessarily severe. But the fact is notoriously otherwise. Whenever the doctor visits a violent or mischievous maniac, however controlling his physiognomy, such patient is always secured by the straight waistcoat; and it is, moreover, thought expedient to afford him the society of one or more keepers.

It has, on some occasions, occurred to me to meet with gentlemen who have imagined themselves eminently gifted with this awful imposition of the eye, but the result has never been satisfactory; for, although I have entertained the fullest confidence of any relation, which such gentlemen might afterwards communicate concerning the success of the experiment, I have never been able to persuade them to practise this rare talent tetè a tetè with a furious lunatic.

However Dr. Pinel may be satisfied of our superiority in this respect, it is but decorous to return the compliment, and if any influence were to be gained over maniacal patients by assumed importance, protracted staring, or a mimicry of fierceness, I verily believe that such pantomime would be much better performed in Paris than in London.

It is to be lamented, that general directions only can be given concerning the management of insane persons; the address, which is acquired by experience and constant intercourse with maniacs, cannot be communicated; it may be learned, but must perish with its possessor. Though man appears to be more distinguished from other animals by the capability he has of transmitting his acquirements to posterity, than by any other attribute of his nature, yet this faculty is deplorably bounded in the finer and more enviable offsprings of human attainment. The happy dexterity of the artisan, the impressive and delighting powers of the actor,

"And every charm of gentler eloquence,
All perishable—like the electric fire,
But strike the frame, and, as they strike, expire."

As most men perceive the faults of others without being aware of their own, so insane people easily detect the nonsense of other madmen, without being able to discover, or even to be made sensible of the incorrect associations of their own ideas. For this reason it is highly important, that he who pretends to regulate the conduct of such patients, should first have learned the management of himself. It should be the great object of the superintendant to gain the confidence of the patient, and to awaken in him respect and obedience; but it will readily be seen, that such confidence, obedience, and respect, can only be procured by superiority of talents, discipline of temper, and dignity of manners. Imbecility, misconduct, and empty consequence, although enforced with the most tyrannical severity, may excite fear, but this will always be mingled with contempt. In speaking of the management of insane persons, it is to be understood that the superintendant must first obtain an ascendency over them. When this is once effected, he will be enabled, on future occasions, to direct and regulate their conduct, according as his better judgment may suggest. He should possess firmness, and, when occasion may require, should exercise his authority in a peremptory manner. He should never threaten but execute; and when the patient has misbehaved, should confine him immediately. As example operates more forcibly than precept, I have found it useful, to order the delinquent to be confined in the presence of the other patients. It displays authority; and the person who has misbehaved becomes awed by the spectators, and more readily submits. It also prevents the wanton exercise of force, and those cruel and unmanly advantages which might be taken when the patient and keeper are shut up in a private room. When the patient is a powerful man, two or more should assist in securing him: by these means it will be easily effected; for, where the force of the contending persons is nearly equal, the mastery cannot be obtained without difficulty and danger.

When the patient is in a furious state, and uncontrolable by kindness and persuasion, he will generally endeavour, by any means, to do as much mischief as possible to the person who opposes him; and instances are not rare where he has overcome the keeper. When the maniac finds his strength, or skill in the contest prevail, he is sure to make the most of such advantage, and the consequence of his victory has sometimes proved fatal to the keeper. On the other hand, it ought to be the object of the keeper to subdue the maniac without doing him any personal injury; and after he has overpowered, to confine him, and thus prevent him from attempting any further mischief. When the patient is a strong man, and highly irritated, it will be impossible for any keeper singly to overcome him without his most forcible exertions, and these cannot be put forth without great violence to the patient. But subduing the maniac, is not the only object, he must afterwards be secured by the straight-waistcoat, or by manacles. It will be seen, that the keeper, who, by the great exertion of his bodily powers, has become faint and exhausted, will be very little in a condition to secure the patient, as his hands must be employed with the implements necessary to confine him; moreover, the patient will have additional strength from the temperate manner, in which he is made to live; whereas, it is but too common, for the keeper to indulge in a diet and beverage, which induce corpulence and difficulty of breathing.[26]

As management is employed to produce a salutary change upon the patient, and to restrain him from committing violence on others and himself; it may here be proper to enquire, upon what occasions, and to what extent, coercion may be used. The term coercion has been understood in a very formidable sense, and not without reason. It has been recommended by very high medical authority to inflict corporal punishment upon maniacs, with a view of rendering them rational, by impressing terror.[27] From Dr. Mead's section on madness it would appear, that in his time flagellation was a common remedy for this disorder. "There is no disease more to be dreaded than madness. For what greater unhappiness can befal a man, than to be deprived of his reason and understanding, to attack his fellow creatures with fury, like a wild beast; to be tied down, *and even beat,*

to prevent his doing mischief to himself or others."—
Medical Precepts and Cautions, page 74.

Dramatic writers abound with allusions to the whip, in the treatment of madness. "Love is meerely a madnesse, and I tel you, deserves as well a darke house, and a whip, as madmen do: and the reason why they are not so punish'd and cured, is, that the Lunacie is so ordinary, that the whippers are in love too."—*As You Like It, act* III. *scene* 2.

Another instance to the same effect may be found in Mr. Dennis's comedy of Jacobite Credulity. *"Bull Junior.* Look you, old gentleman, I will touch this matter as gently as I can to you. Your friends taking notice, that you were grown something foolish, whimsical, absurd, and so forth, thought fit to have you sent to the College here, [Bedlam] that you might go through a course of philosophy, and be cudgel'd and firk'd into a little wisdom, by the surly Professors of this place."—*Select Works, vol.* ii. *p.* 363. And again, in the next page; "If thou canst give but so much as a reasonable answer to any thing; if thou either knowest what thou art, or where thou art, or with whom thou art, then will I be contented to be thought mad, and dieted and flogged in thy stead."

It also appears from Mr. Douce's valuable dissertation, that the domesticated fool frequently underwent a similar castigation, to curb the licentiousness of his discourse, or, as a punishment for the obscenity of his actions. Indeed this system of corporal chastisement seems to have been general, and may afford some apology for introducing, from a very rare little book, an account of the manner of treating this malady in Constantinople, about the middle of the 16th century.[28]

"Of a place called Timarahane for the Correction of the Insane.

"The sultan Bajazet caused a building to be erected for the reception of insane persons, in order, that they might not wander about the city, and there exhibit their mad pranks. This building is constructed in the manner of an hospital: there are about an hundred and fifty keepers appointed to look after them; they are likewise furnished with medicines and other necessary articles. These keepers, armed with cudgels, patrole the city in search of the insane; and when they discover such, they secure them by the neck and hands with an iron chain, and, by dint of the cudgel, convey them to Timarahane. On entering this place, they are confined by the neck, with a much larger chain, which is fixed into the wall, and comes over their bed place, so that they are kept chained in their beds. In general, about forty are confined there, at some distance from each other.

"They are frequently visited by the people of the city, as a species of amusement. The keepers constantly stand over them with cudgels; for, if left to themselves, they would spoil and destroy their beds and hurl the tables at each other. At the times of giving them food, the keepers examine them, and, if they notice any, who are disorderly, they beat them severely; but, if they should by accident, find any, who no longer exhibit symptoms of insanity, they treat them with greater regard."

What success may have followed such disgraceful and inhuman treatment, I have not yet learned; nor should I be desirous of meeting with any one, who could give me the information.

If the patient be so far deprived of understanding, as to be insensible why he is punished, such correction, setting aside its cruelty, is manifestly absurd: and, if his state be such, as to be conscious of the impropriety of his conduct, there are other methods more mild and effectual. Would any rational practitioner, in a case of phrenitis, or in the delirium of fever, order his patient to be scourged? he would rather suppose, that the brain, or its membranes, were inflamed, and that the incoherence of discourse and violence of action were produced by such local disease. It has been shewn by the preceding dissections, that the contents of the cranium, in all the instances that have occurred to me, have been in a morbid state. It should, therefore, be the object of the practitioner, to remove such disease, rather than irritate and torment the sufferer.—Coercion should only be considered as a protecting and salutary restraint.

In the most violent state of the disease, the patient should be kept alone in a dark and quiet room, so that he may not be affected by the stimuli of light or sound, such abstraction more readily disposing to sleep. As in this violent state there is a strong propensity to associate ideas, it is particularly important to prevent the accession of such as might be transmitted through the medium of the senses. The hands should be properly secured, and the patient should also be confined by one leg; this will prevent him from committing any violence. The more effectual and convenient mode of confining the hands is by metallic manacles; for, should the patient, as frequently occurs, be constantly endeavouring to liberate himself, the friction of the skin against a polished metallic body may be long sustained without injury; whereas excoriation shortly takes place when the surface is rubbed with linen or cotton. Ligatures should on all occasions be avoided. The straight waistcoat is admirably calculated to prevent patients from doing mischief to themselves; but in the furious state, and particularly in warm weather, it irritates, and increases that restlessness which patients of this description usually labour under. They then disdain the incumbrance of clothing, and seem to delight in exposing their bodies to the atmosphere. Where the patient is in a condition to be sensible of restraint, he may be punished for improper behaviour, by confining him to his room, by degrading him, and not allowing him to associate with the convalescents, and by withholding certain indulgences, he had been accustomed to enjoy.

In speaking of coercion, I cannot avoid reprobating a practice, which has prevailed in some private receptacles for the insane, but which, it is presumed, will henceforward be discontinued. I mean, the practice of half-stifling a noisy patient, by placing a pillow before the mouth, and forcibly pressing upon it, so as to stop respiration. It is unnecessary to enquire, how such wanton cruelty came to be introduced; it must have been the suggestion of ignorance, and the perpetration of savageness and brutality. Sighs, tears, sobs, and exclamations, are the unaffected language of passion, and come kindly to our relief, in states of sorrow and alarm. Indeed, they appear to be the natural remedies, to

"Cleanse the stufft bosom of that perillous stuffe, Which weighs upon the heart."

The mild and rational practice of Bethlem Hospital, tolerates these involuntary ejaculations. It is there considered, that a noisy and loquacious maniac, has not the power to control his utterance of sounds, which, from the habitual connexion between ideas and speech, must necessarily follow. It is there only viewed as a symptom, or part of the disorder; and that, if the cause cannot be suppressed, the effect should not be punished.

As madmen frequently entertain very high, and even romantic notions of honour, they are often rendered much more tractable by wounding their pride, than by severity of discipline.

Speaking of the effects of management, on a very extensive scale, I can truly declare, that by gentleness of manner, and kindness of treatment, I have seldom failed to obtain the confidence, and conciliate the esteem of insane persons, and have succeeded by these means in procuring from them respect and obedience. There are certainly some patients who are not to be trusted, and in whom malevolence forms the prominent feature of their character: such persons should always be kept under a certain restraint, but this is not incompatible with kindness and humanity.

It would, in this part of the work, be particularly gratifying to my feelings if I could develope this *English secret* for the moral management of the insane, which has been so ardently, yet unsuccessfully sought after by Dr. Pinel. For fourteen years I have been daily in the habit of visiting a very considerable number of madmen, and of mixing indiscriminately among them, without ever having received a blow or personal insult. During this time I have always gone alone, and have never found the necessity for the assistance or protection of a keeper. The superintendant of the Bicêtre, according to Dr. Pinel's account, is usually attended by his keepers, [gens de service] though he is said to possess[29] "une fermeté inébranlable, un courage raisonné et soutenu par des qualités physiques les plus propres á imposer, une stature de corps bien proportionnée, des membres pleins de force et de vigeur, et dans des momens orageux le ton de voix le plus foudroyant, la contenance la plus fiére et la plus intrepide." Not being myself endowed with any of these rare qualities; carrying no thunder in my voice, nor lightning in my eye, it has been requisite for me to have recourse to other expedients. In the first place, it has been thought proper to devote some time and attention to discover the character of the patient, and to ascertain wherein, and on what points, his insanity consists: it is also important to learn the history of his disorder, from his relatives and friends, and to enquire particularly respecting any violence he may have attempted towards himself or others.

In holding conferences with patients in order to discover their insanity, no advantage has ever been derived from assuming a magisterial importance, or by endeavouring to stare them out of countenance: a mildness of manner and expression, an attention to their narrative, and seeming acquiescence in its truth, succeed much better. By such conduct they acquire confidence in the practitioner; and if he will have patience, and not too frequently interrupt them, they will soon satisfy his mind as to the derangement of their intellects.

When a patient is admitted into Bethlem Hospital, if he be sufficiently rational to profit by such tuition, it is explained to him, by the keepers and convalescents, that he is to be obedient to the officers of the house, and especially to myself, with whom he will have daily intercourse; they point out to him, that all proper indulgences will be allowed to good behaviour, and that seclusion and coercion instantly succeed to disobedience and revolt. As *nemo repente turpissimus*, so no one in an instant, from a state of tranquillity, becomes furiously mad: the precursory symptoms are manifold and successive, and allow of sufficient time to secure the patient before mischief ensues; it is principally by taking these precautions that our patients are observed to be so orderly and obedient. The examples of those who are under strict coercion, being constantly in view, operate more forcibly on their minds than any precepts which the most consummate wisdom could suggest. In this moral management, the co-operation of the convalescents is particularly serviceable; they consider themselves in a state of probation, and, in order to be liberated, are anxious, by every attention and assistance, to convince the superintendants of their restoration to sanity of mind. From mildness of treatment, and confidence reposed in them, they become attached, and are always disposed to give information concerning any projected mischief.

Considering how much we are the creatures of habit, it might naturally be hoped, and experience justifies the expectation, that madmen might be benefited by bringing their actions into a system of regularity. It might be supposed, that as thought precedes action, that whenever the ideas are incoherent, the actions will also be irregular. Most probably they would be so, if uncontroled; but custom, confirmed into habit, destroys this natural propensity, and renders them correct in their behaviour, though they still remain equally depraved in their intellects.

We have a number of patients in Bethlem Hospital, whose ideas are in the most disordered state, who yet act, upon ordinary occasions, with great steadiness and propriety, and are capable of being trusted to a considerable extent. A fact of such importance in the history of the human mind, might lead us to hope, that by superinducing different habits of thinking, the irregular associations would be corrected.

It is impossible to effect this suddenly, or by reasoning, for madmen can never be convinced of the folly of their opinions. Their belief in them is firmly fixed, and cannot be shaken. The more frequently these opinions are recurred to, under a conviction of their truth, the deeper they subside in the mind, and become more obstinately entangled:[30] the object should therefore be to prevent such recurrence by occupying the mind on different subjects, and thus diverting it from the favorite and accustomed train of ideas.

As I have been induced to suppose, from the appearances on dissection, that the immediate cause of this disease probably consists in a morbid affection of the brain, it may be inferred, that all modes of cure by reasoning, or conducting the current of thought into different channels, must be ineffectual, so long as such local disease shall continue. It is, however, likely that insanity is often continued by habit; that incoherent associations, frequently recurred to, become received as truths, in the same manner as a tale, which, although untrue, by being repeatedly told, shall be credited at last by the narrator, as if it had certainly happened. It should likewise be observed, that these incorrect associations of ideas are acquired in the same way as just ones are formed, and that such are as likely to remain as the most accurate opinions. The generality of minds are very little capable of tracing the origin of their ideas; there are many opinions we are in possession of, with the history and acquisition of which, we are totally unacquainted. We see this in a remarkable manner in patients who are recovering from their insanity: they will often say such appearances have been presented to my mind, with all the force and reality of truth: I saw them as plainly as I now behold any other object, and can hardly be persuaded that they did not occur. It also does not unfrequently happen, that patients will declare, that certain notions are forced into their minds, of which they see the folly and incongruity, and yet complain that they cannot prevent their intrusion.

As the patient should be taught to view the medical superintendant as a superior person, the latter should be particularly cautious never to deceive him. Madmen are generally more hurt at deception than punishment; and, whenever they detect the imposition, never fail to lose that confidence and respect which they ought to entertain for the person who governs them.

In the moral management of the insane, this circumstance cannot be too strongly impressed on the mind of the practitioner: and those persons, who have had the greatest experience in this department of medical science, concur in this opinion. The late Dr. John Monro expressly says, "The physician should never deceive them in *any* thing, but more especially with regard to their distemper; for as they are generally conscious of it themselves, they acquire a kind of reverence for those who know it; and by letting them see, that he is thoroughly acquainted with their complaint, he may very often gain such an ascendant over them, that they will readily follow his directions."[31]

Very different directions are, however, issued by a late writer,[32] and which, on account of their novelty, contrivance, and singular morality, deserve the consideration of the reader.

"The *conscientious physician*, in the execution of his duty, attempting the removal of these deplorable maladies, is under the necessity of occasionally deviating from the accustomed routine of practice, of stepping out of the beaten track, and, in some cases, that have resisted the usual methods, is warranted in adopting any others, that have *only* the slightest *plausibility*, or that promise the smallest hope of success. Thus, the employment of what may be termed *pious frauds*: as when *one* simple erroneous idea stamps the character of the disease, depriving the affected party of the common enjoyments of society, though capable of reasoning with propriety, perhaps, with ingenuity, on every subject, not connected with that of his hallucination, the correction of which has resisted our very best exertions, and, where there is no obvious corporeal indisposition, it certainly is allowable to try the effect of certain deceptions, contrived to make strong impressions on the senses, by means of *unexpected, unusual, striking*, or apparently *supernatural* agents; such as after waking the party from sleep, either suddenly or by a gradual process, by *imitated thunder*, or soft music, according to the peculiarity of the case; *combating* the erroneous deranged notion, either by some *pointed sentence*, or signs *executed in phosphorus* upon the wall of the bed chamber; or by some *tale, assertion*, or *reasoning*; by one in the character of an *angel, prophet*, or *devil*: but the actor in this drama must possess much *skill, and be very perfect in his part*."

It is of great service to establish a system of regularity in the actions of insane people. They should be made to rise, take exercise, and food, at stated times. Independently of such regularity contributing to health, it also renders them much more easily manageable.

Concerning their diet, it is merely necessary to observe, that it should be light, and easy of digestion. The proper quantity must be directed by the good sense of the superintendant, according to the age and vigour of the patient, and proportioned to the degree of bodily exercise he may be in the habit of using; "but they should never be suffered to live too low, especially while they are under a course of physic."[33] To my knowledge, no experiments have yet been instituted respecting the diet of insane persons: they have never been compelled to live entirely on farinaceous substances. The diet of Bethlem Hospital allows animal food three times a week, and on the other days bread with cheese, or occasionally butter, together with milk pottage, rice milk, &c. Those who are regarded as incurable patients ought certainly to be indulged in a greater latitude of diet, but this should never be permitted to border on intemperance. To those who are in circumstances to afford such comforts, wine may be allowed in moderation, and the criterion of the proper quantity, will be that which does not affect the temper of the lunatic, that which does not exasperate his aversions, or render his philosophy obtrusive. Although it seems rational in all states of madness, that temperance should be strictly enjoined, yet an author of the present day[34] steps out of the trodden path, and seriously advises us, in difficult cases, to drown lunacy in intoxication; and, strange as it may appear, has taught us to await the feast of Reason from the orgies of Bacchus. "The conversion of religious melancholy into furious madness is a frequent occurrence, and is generally followed by recovery. This has suggested the *propriety*, in some cases that have resisted more common means, of producing a degree of excitement by means of stimuli, in fact, *keeping the patient for days in succession in a state of intoxication*, which has often occasioned an alleviation of symptoms, and sometimes *restored the sufferers to reason*."

Confinement is always necessary in cases of insanity, and should be enforced as early in the disease as possible. By confinement, it is to be understood that the patient should be removed from home. During his continuance at his own house he can never be kept in a tranquil state. The interruptions of his family, the loss of the accustomed obedience of his servants, and the idea of being under restraint, in a place where he considers himself the master, will be constant sources of irritation to his mind. It is also known, from considerable experience, that of those patients who have remained under the immediate care of their relatives and friends, very few have recovered. Even the visits of their friends, when they are violently disordered, are productive of great inconvenience, as they are always more unquiet and ungovernable for some time afterwards. It is a well-known fact, that they are less disposed to acquire a dislike to those who are strangers, than to those with whom they have been intimately acquainted; they become therefore less dangerous, and are more easily restrained. It ought to be understood that no interruption to this discipline should defeat its salutary operation. On this account more patients recover in a public hospital, than in a private house, appropriated for the reception of lunatics. In the former, the superintendants persist in a plan laid down, and seldom deviate from their established rules: such asylum being a place of charitable relief, they are indifferent about pleasing the friends and relatives of the patient, who cannot there intrude to visit them at their option. In a private receptacle emolument is the first object, and however wisely they may have formed their regulations, they soon feel themselves subordinate to the caprice and authority of those by whom they are paid.

It frequently happens, that patients who have been brought immediately from their families, and who were said to be in a violent and ferocious state at home, become suddenly calm and tractable when placed in the hospital. On the other hand it is equally certain, that there are many patients whose disorder speedily recurs after having been suffered to return to their families, although they have for a length of time conducted themselves, under confinement, in a very orderly manner. When they are in a convalescent state the occasional visits of their friends are attended with manifest advantage. Such an intercourse imparts consolation, and presents views of future happiness and comfort. But certain restrictions should be imposed on the visits of these friends; ignorant people often, after a few minutes conversation with the patient, will suppose him perfectly recovered, and acquaint him with their opinion: this induces him to suppose that he is well, and he frequently becomes impatient of confinement and restraint. From such improper intercourse I have known many patients relapse, and in two instances I have a well-founded suspicion that it excited attempts at suicide.

Many patients have received considerable benefit by change of situation, which occupies the mind with new objects, and this sometimes takes place very shortly after the removal.

"Haply the Seas and Countries different
With variable objects, shall expell
This something setled matter in his heart:
Whereon his Braines still beating, puts him thus
From fashion of himselfe."

In what particular cases, or stages of the disease, this may be recommended, I am not enabled, by sufficient experience, to determine.

CHAP. VIII.

REMEDIES FOR INSANITY.

Bleeding.

WHERE the patient is strong, and of a plethoric habit, and where the disorder has not been of any long continuance, bleeding has been found of considerable advantage, and as far as I have yet observed, is the most beneficial remedy that has been employed. The melancholic cases have been equally relieved with the maniacal by this mode of treatment. Venesection by the arm is, however, inferior in its good effects to blood taken from the head by cupping. This operation, performed in the manner to which I have been accustomed, consists in having the head previously shaven, and six or eight cupping glasses applied on the scalp. By these means any quantity of blood may be taken, and in as short a time, as by an orifice made in a vein by the lancet. When the raving paroxysm has continued for a considerable time, and the scalp has become unusually flaccid; or where a stupid state has succeeded to violence of considerable duration, no benefit has been derived from bleeding: indeed these states are generally attended by a degree of bodily weakness, sufficient to prohibit such practice independently of other considerations.

The quantity of blood to be taken, must be left to the discretion of the practitioner: from eight to sixteen ounces may be drawn, and the operation occasionally repeated, as circumstances may require.

In some cases where blood was drawn at the commencement of the disease from the arm, and from patients who were extremely furious and ungovernable, it was covered with a buffy coat; but in other cases it has seldom or never such an appearance. In more than two hundred patients, male and female, who were let blood by venesection, there were only six whose blood could be termed sizy.

In some few instances hemoptysis has preceded convalescence, as has also a bleeding from the hemorrhoidal veins. Epistaxis has not, to my knowledge, ever occurred.

Before particular remedies, to be employed for the cure of mania and melancholia, are recommended, it may be necessary to give some directions concerning the means to be used for their certain administration.

Maniacs in general feel a great aversion to become benefited from those medicinal preparations which practitioners employ for their relief; and on many occasions they refuse them altogether. Presuming that some good is to be procured by the operation of medicines on persons so affected, and aware of their propensity to reject them, it becomes a proper object of enquiry how such salutary agents may most securely, and with the least disadvantage, be conveyed into the stomachs of these refractory subjects. For the attainment of this end various instruments have been contrived, but that which has been more frequently employed, and is the most destructive and devilish engine of this set of apparatus, is termed a *spouting* boat. It will not be necessary to fatigue the reader with a particular description of this coarse tool, except to remark, that it is constructed somewhat like a child's pap boat; and is intended to force an entrance into the mouth through the barriers of the teeth.[35]

In those cases, where patients have been obstinately bent on starving themselves, or where they have become determined to resist the introduction of remedies calculated for their relief, I have always been enabled to convey both into their stomachs, at any time, and in any quantity that might be necessary, by the employment of an instrument, of which the figure and dimensions are here given.

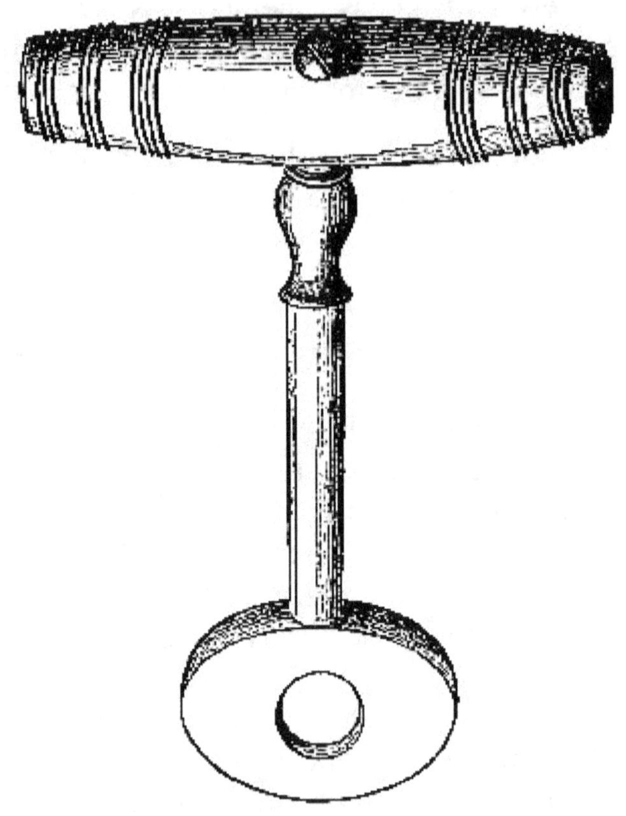

Since the use of this very simple and efficient instrument, which I constructed about twelve years ago, I can truly affirm, that no patient has ever been deprived of a tooth, and that the food or remedy has always been conveyed into the stomach of the patient.

The manner in which this compulsory operation is performed, consists in placing the head of the patient between the knees of the person who is to use the instrument: a second assistant secures the hands, (if the straight-waistcoat be not employed) and a third keeps down the legs. As soon as the mouth is opened, the instrument may be introduced; it presses down the tongue, and keeps the jaws sufficiently asunder to admit of the introduction of the medicine, which should be contained in a vial, or tin pot with a spout, to allow it to run in a small stream. The nose of the patient being held by the left hand of the person who uses the instrument, a small quantity of the medicine is to be poured into the mouth, and when deglutition has commenced, is to be repeated, so as to continue the act of swallowing until the whole be taken.

A little address will obviate the determination of the patient to keep his teeth closed: he may be blindfolded at the commencement, which never fails to alarm him, and urges him to enquire what the persons around him are about: causing him to sneeze, by a pinch of snuff, always opens the mouth previously to that convulsion, or tickling the nose with a feather commonly produces the same effect.

With delicate females, where one or more of the grinder-teeth are wanting, the finger may be introduced on the inside of the cheek, which being strongly pressed outwards will prevent the patient from biting, and form a sufficient cavity to pour in the liquid. With a wish of speaking confidently on this subject, I have usually performed the business of forcing, more especially amongst the females, and it has, in some degree, rewarded my trouble; it has ascertained the practicability of administering remedies; and it has also afforded the consolation, that, where the means employed have produced no good, the patient has sustained no injury.

An opinion has long prevailed, that mad people are particularly constipated, and likewise extremely difficult to be purged. From all the observations I have been able to make, insane patients, on the contrary, are of very delicate and irritable bowels, and are well, and copiously purged, by a common cathartic draught. That, which has been commonly employed at the hospital, was prepared agreeably to the following formula:

℞. Infusi sennæ ℥iss ad ℥ij.

Tincturæ sennæ ʒi ad ʒij.

Syrupi spinæ cervinæ ʒi ad ʒij.

but, within the last seven years, the tinctura jalapij has been substituted for the tinctura sennæ. It is so far an improvement, that it operates more speedily, and produces less griping.

This medicine seldom fails of procuring four or five stools, and frequently a greater number.

In confirmation of what I have advanced, respecting the irritable state of the intestines in mad people, it may be mentioned, that the ordinary complaints, with which they are affected, are diarrhœa and dysentery: these have heretofore been very violent and obstinate.

Perhaps it may be attributed to superior care that the occurrence of these complaints has, of late years, been comparatively rare, contrasted with the numbers who were formerly attacked with such diseases; and, when they do happen, an improved method of treatment has rendered these intestinal affections no longer formidable or fatal.

In those very violent diarrhœas, which ordinarily terminate in dysentery, from five to ten grains of the pilula hydrargyri have been given according to the sex, constitution, and nature of the complaint, once or twice a day, and with general success.

It may be necessary to add, that it is proper, during the course of this mercurial remedy, which shortly arrests the disease, to keep the bowels in an open state, by some of the milder purgatives employed every third or fourth day.

Diarrhœa very often proves a natural cure of insanity; at least, there is sufficient reason to suppose, that such evacuation has very much contributed to it. The number of cases, which might be adduced in confirmation of this remark, is considerable; and the speedy convalescence, after such evacuation, is still more remarkable.

In many cases of insanity there prevails a great degree of insensibility, so that patients have scarcely appeared to feel the passing of setons, the drawing of blisters, or the punctures of cupping. On many occasions, I have known the urine retained for a considerable time, without complaint from the patient, although it is well ascertained, that there is no affection more painful and distressing than distension of the bladder.

Of this general insensibility the intestinal canal may be supposed to partake; but this is not commonly the case; and, if it should frequently prevail, would be widely different from a particular and exclusive torpor of the primæ viæ.

But, sometimes, there arises a state of disease in maniacs, where the stomach and intestines are particularly inert. The patient refuses to take food, and is obstinately constipated: the tongue is foul, and the skin is tinged with a yellowish hue: the eyes assume a glossy lustre, and exhibit a peculiar wildness. In this state, I have given two drachms of the pulvis jalapij for a dose, and which, on some occasions, has procured but one stool, so that it has been necessary several times to repeat the same quantity. After the bowels have been sufficiently evacuated, the appetite commonly returns, and the patient takes food as usual.

Much mischief may be produced, if it be attempted to force food into the stomach in such a case, which the ignorance of keepers may attempt, supposing it to originate in the obstinacy of the patient. In order to continue the bowels in a relaxed state, after they have been sufficiently emptied of their contents, the following formula has been employed with advantage:

R. Infusi sennæ, ℥vijss

    Kali Tartarizati, ℥ss

    Antimonij Tartarizati, gr 1ss

    Tincturæ jalapij, ℨij

From two to three table spoonsful may be given once or twice a day, as occasion may require.

There are some circumstances unconnected with disease of mind, which might dispose insane persons to costiveness. I now speak of such as are confined, and who come more directly under our observation. When they are mischievously disposed they require a greater degree of restraint, and are consequently deprived of that air and exercise which so much contribute to regularity of bowels. It is well known that those who have been in the habits of free living, and who come suddenly to a more temperate diet, are very much disposed to costiveness. But to adduce the fairest proof of what has been advanced, I can truly state, that incurable patients, who have for many years been confined in the Hospital, are subject to no inconveniences from constipation. Many patients are averse to food, and where little is taken in, the egesta must be inconsiderable.

To return from this digression: it is concluded, from very ample experience, that cathartic medicines are of the greatest service, and ought to be considered as an indispensable remedy in cases of insanity. The good sense and experience of every practitioner must direct him as to the dose, and frequency with which these means are to be employed, and of the occasions where they would be prejudicial.

Vomiting.

However strongly this practice may have been recommended, and how much soever it may at present prevail, I am sorry that it is not in my power to speak of it favourably. In many instances, and in some where blood-letting had been previously employed, paralytic affections have within a few hours supervened on the exhibition of an emetic, more especially where the patient has been of a full habit, and has had the appearance of an increased determination to the head.

It has been for many years the practice of Bethlem Hospital to administer to the curable patients four or five emetics in the spring of the year; but, on consulting my book of cases, I have not found that such patients have been particularly benefited by the use of this remedy. From one grain and half to two grains of tartarized antimony has been the usual dose, which has hardly ever failed of procuring full vomiting. In the few instances where the plan of exhibiting this medicine in nauseating doses was pursued for a considerable time, it by no means answered the expectations which had been raised in its favour by very high authority. Where the tartarized antimony, given with this intention, operated as a purgative, it generally produced beneficial effects.

Ten years have elapsed since the former edition of this work appeared; but this length of time, and subsequent observation, have not enabled me to place any greater confidence in the operation of emetics, as a cure for insanity.

An author[36] who has lately published a work, entitled *"Practical Observations on Insanity,"* is however a determined fautor of emetics in maniacal cases. In his skilful hands they have worked marvellous cures; nor have any prejudicial effects ever resulted from their employment. Perhaps no one has enjoyed a fairer opportunity of witnessing the effects of remedies for insane persons than myself; and when emetics are employed in Bethlem Hospital they have the best chance of effecting all the relief they are competent to afford, as they are given by themselves, without the intervention of other medicines; and this course of emetics usually continues six weeks. Had Dr. Cox confined himself to the relation of his own victories in combating madness with vomits, it would have been sufficient; but he endeavours to raise the leveé en masse of medical opinion to co-operate with his sentiments. He says, page 78, "Yet *every* physician, who has devoted his attention to this branch of the profession, *must* differ from him when he treats of vomiting." It was never my intention to deny, in a disordered state of the stomach, that the madman would be equally benefited with one in his senses by the operation of a vomit: but I have asserted, that after the administration of many thousand emetics to persons who were insane, but otherwise in good health, that I never saw any benefit derived from their use. It will also be granted, that some ascendancy may be gained over a furious maniac by forcing him to take a vomit, or any other medicine, but this is widely different from any positive advantage resulting from the act of vomiting. Sir John Colebatch, in his *"Dissertation concerning Misletoe,"* says, *p.* 35, "But I have been for some years afraid of giving vomits, even of the gentlest sort, in convulsive distempers, from some terrible accidents, that have been likely to ensue, from moderate doses of Ipecacuanha itself."

In St. Luke's hospital, the largest public receptacle for insane persons, where the medical treatment is directed by a physician of the highest character and eminence, and whose experience is, at least, equal to that of any professional man in this country, vomits are by no means considered as the order of the day; they may be employed to remove symptoms concomitant with madness, but are not held as specifics for this disease.

In reading over the cases related by Dr. Cox, there is no one, where emetics have been solely employed as agents of cure; they have been always linked with other remedies; and it requires more sagacity than even the doctor can exact, to pronounce, when different means of cure are combined, to which the palm should be adjudged. In the relation of my own experience concerning vomiting, as a remedy for insanity, I have had only in view the communication of facts, for I entertain neither partiality nor aversion to any remedies, beyond the fair claim which their operations possess. Had I modestly ventured to state, after the example of the Doctor, "that I had *devoted* myself *exclusively* and *assiduously* for a *series of years*, to the care of insane patients in an *establishment*, where persons of *both sexes* are received,"[37] it might be suspected, that the superstructure of my philosophy had been reared on the basis of private emolument.

Camphor.

This remedy has been highly extolled, and doubtless with reason, by those who have recommended it: my own experience merely extends to ten cases; a number, from which no decisive inference of its utility ought to be drawn. The dose was gradually increased, from five grains to two drachms, twice a day; and, in nine cases, the use of this remedy was continued for the space of two months. Of the patients, to whom the camphor was given, only two recovered: one of these had no symptoms of convalescence for several months after the use of this remedy had been abandoned: the other, a melancholic patient, certainly mended during the time he was taking it; but he was never able to bear more than ten grains thrice a day. He complained that it made him feel as if he were intoxicated. Considering the insoluble nature of camphor, and the impracticability of compelling a lunatic to swallow a pill or bolus, it has been found convenient (when a large quantity was required) to give this medicine in the form of an emulsion, by dissolving the camphor in hot olive oil, and afterwards adding a sufficient quantity of warm water and aqua ammoniæ puræ.

Cold Bathing.

This remedy having for the most part been employed, in conjunction with others, it becomes difficult to ascertain how far it may be exclusively beneficial in this disease. The instances where it has been separately used for the cure of insanity, are too few to enable me to draw any satisfactory conclusions. I may, however, safely relate, that in many instances, paralytic affections have in a few hours supervened on cold bathing, especially where the patient has been in a furious state, and of a plethoric habit. That this is not unlikely to happen may be supposed from the difficulty of compelling the patient to go head-foremost into the bath. In some cases vertigo, and in others a considerable degree of fever ensued after immersion. The shower-bath was employed some years ago in the hospital, and many cases were selected in order to give a fair trial to this remedy, but I am unable to say, that any considerable advantage was derived to the patients from its use. If I might be permitted to give an opinion on this subject, the principal benefit resulting from this remedy, has been in the latter stages of the disease, and when the system had been previously lowered by evacuations. As a remedy for insanity cold bathing has been disregarded by a celebrated practitioner. To a question from a select committee of the House of Commons to Doctor Willis, 9th March, 1807, the following answer was given.

Question. Are you of opinion that warm and cold baths are necessary for lunatic patients?

Answer. I think warm baths may be very useful, but it *can seldom happen* that a cold bath will be required.[38]

Blisters.

These have been in several cases applied to the head, and a very copious discharge maintained for many days, but without any manifest advantage. The late Dr. John Monro, who had, perhaps, seen more cases of this disease than any other practitioner, and who, joined to his extensive experience, possessed the talent of accurate observation, mentions, that he "never saw the least good effect of blisters in madness, unless it was at the beginning, while there was some degree of fever, or when they have been applied to particular symptoms accompanying this complaint."[39] Dr. Mead also concurs in this opinion. "Blistering plasters applied to the head will possibly be thought to deserve a place among the remedies of this disease, but I have often found them do more harm than good by their over great irritation."—*Medical Precepts, page* 94. Although blisters appear to be of little service, when put on the head, yet I have, in many cases, seen much good result from applying them to the legs. In patients who have continued for some time in a very furious state, and where evacuations have been sufficiently employed, large blisters applied to the inside of the legs, have often, and within a short time, mitigated the violence of the disorder.

In a few cases setons have been employed, but no benefit has been derived from their use, although the discharge was continued above two months.

Respecting opium, it may be observed, that whenever it has been exhibited, during a violent paroxysm, it has hardly ever procured sleep: but, on the contrary, has rendered those who have taken it much more furious: and, where it has for a short time produced rest, the patient has, after its operation, awaked in a state of increased violence.

Many of the tribe of narcotic poisons have been recommended for the cure of madness; but, my own experience of those remedies is very limited, nor is it my intention to make further trials. Other, and perhaps whimsical modes of treating this disorder, have been mentioned: whirling,[40] or spinning a madman round, on a pivot, has been gravely proposed; and, music has been extolled, with a considerable glow of imagination, by the same gentleman.—That the medical student may be fully aware of the manifold agents which *practical physicians* have suggested for the restoration of reason, I shall conclude my volume with the following extract.[41]

"The medical philosopher, in his study of human nature, must have observed, that *sympathetic correspondence of action* between the mind and body, which is *uniformly* present in health and disease, though *varying* with circumstances. The different passions, according to their nature, the degree or intensity of application, and the sensibility of the party, exhibit certain characteristic expressions of countenance, and produce obvious *changes*, actions, or motions, in the animal economy. Music has been found to occasion *all* these actions, changes, and movements, in some sensible systems; and where one passion morbidly predominates, as frequently happens in mania, those species of simple or combined sounds, *capable of exciting an opposite passion*, may be *very usefully* employed. *If* then such effects *can* be produced by such a power, acting on a mind only endued with its healthy proportion of susceptibility, what may we *not* expect where the sensibility is morbidly increased, and where the patient is alive to the most minute impressions? Cases frequently occur where such acuteness of sensibility, and *extreme* delicacy of system exist, that most of the more common, *moral*, and medical means are contra-indicated; *here* relief may be often administered through the medium of the *senses*; the *varied modulations, the lulling, soothing* cords of even an Eölian harp have *appeased* contending passions, *allayed* miserable feeling, and afforded ease and tranquillity to the bosom *tortured* with real or fancied woe: and I can easily *imagine*, that *jarring discord, grating harsh rending* sounds, applied to an ear *naturally* musical, would uniformly excite great commotion. Under circumstances calculated to assist this action, by producing unpleasant impressions through the medium of the other senses, as when SCREECHES and YELLS are made in an apartment painted *black* and *red*, or *glaring white*, every man must be painfully affected: the maniacal patient, *however torpid, must* be roused: or, on the contrary, where an opposite state obtains, extreme sensibility and impatience of powerful impression, there *much may be expected* from placing the patient in an *airy room*, surrounded with *flowers breathing odours*, the walls and furniture *coloured green*, and the air agitated by undulations of the softest harmony. *Much* of this may appear FANCIFUL and RIDICULOUS, but the *enquiring* practitioner *will* find, on making the experiment, it deserves his *serious* attention; and no mean is to be despised that is capable of arresting the attention, changing the trains of thought, interesting the affections, removing or diminishing painful sensations, and ultimately rendering both mind and body sensible to impressions, and *all this has been effected by music*. Every individual is not capable of accurately estimating the *extensive powers* of this agent; but I would ask the *musical amateur*, or the *experienced professor*, if he have not frequently felt sensations the most *exquisite* and *indescribable*; if he have not experienced the whole frame *trilling* with *inexpressible delight*, when the *tide* of full harmony has FLOWN on his ear, and the most *wretched miserable* feeling, UNIVERSAL HORRIPILATIO and CUTIS ANSERINA from the *grating crash* of discord? All the varied sensations from transport to disgust, have been occasioned by the different movements in one piece of music. I might *amuse* my readers with a great variety of instances where persons have been very singularly affected by means of music, and where its powers have extended to the *brute creation*, but this I purposely avoid."

FINIS.

Footnotes:

[1] The choice of these words must be left to the taste of the reader, Dr. Johnson not having thought proper to admit them into his dictionary.

[2] Some doubts are entertained whether Dr. Boord was physician to King Henry the eighth, but he was certainly a fellow of the College.

[3] Apprehension of sensations. This is perhaps only an endeavour to explain the thing, *by* the thing, or producing words of similar import with different sounds. Junius, speaking of the word hand (as derived from the gothic Handus) says, "Quidam olim deduxerunt vocabulum ab antiquo verbo HENDO, *Capio*: unde Prehendo, APPREHENDO, &c."—*Gothicum Glossarium*, p. 188. Professor Ihre conceives it equally probable that the old latin word *hendo* may have had a northern origin. "Id vero non possum, quin addam, oppidó mihi probabile fieri, ipsammet hanc vocem latio olim peregrinam non fuisse, quod quippe augurar ex derivato HENDO, capio, unde prehendo cum derivatis pullularunt."—*Glossarium Sviogothicum. tom.* i. *p.* 778.

[4] Quere. Why should the most *active* characteristics of our nature be termed *Passions*? The word seems properly employed in *Passion week*, the period commemorative of Christ's suffering or *Passion*. But we are said to *fly*, or *fall* into a passion, and then passion *gets the better of us*. For the softer sex we conceive the most delicate, refined, and honorable *passion*, yet every one allows the dreadful consequences which ensue from an indulgence of our *passions*, and most persons agree that *passion*, carried to excess, constitutes madness—we live in a world of metaphor.

[5] In many instances, although it is far from being general, pain of the head, and throbbing of its arteries precede an attack of insanity; sometimes giddiness is complained of as a precursory symptom. Those who have been several times disordered, are now and then sensible of the approaching return of their malady. Some have stated, a sense of working in the head, and also in the intestines, as if they were in a state of fermentation. Others observe that they do not seem to possess their natural feelings, but they all agree that they feel confused from the sudden and rapid intrusion of unconnected thoughts.

[6] To illustrate how necessarily our sensations, or ideas must become confused, when their succession is too rapid, the relation of some experiments on that subject will sufficiently conduce.

"But by the able assistance of Mr. Herschel, I am in a condition to give some approximation, at least, towards ascertaining the velocity of our audible sensations. For having, by means of a clock, produced sounds, which succeeded each other with such rapidity, that the intervals between each of them were (as far as could be judged) the smallest posible; he found he could evidently distinguish one hundred and sixty of them to flow in a second of time. Now as each interval must in this case be reckoned as a sensation likewise, as it might be filled up with a sound thereby making it a continued one; it follows, that we are capable of entertaining at least three hundred and twenty audible sensations in that period of time."—*Vide a Treatise on Time, by W. Watson, Jun. M. D. F. R. S. 8vo, 1785, page 32.*

[7] The late Dr. Johnson was remarkably distinguished by certain peculiarities of action when his mind was deeply engaged. Sir Joshua Reynolds was of opinion "that it proceeded from a habit he had indulged himself in, of

accompanying his thoughts with certain untoward actions." "One instance of his absence, and particularity as it is characteristic of the man, may be worth relating. When he and I took a journey into the West, we visited the late Mr. Banks, of Dorsetshire; the conversation turning upon pictures, which Johnson could not well see, he retired to a corner of the room, stretching out his right leg as far as he could reach before him, then bringing up his left leg, and stretching his right still further on. The old gentleman observing him, went up to him, and in a very courteous manner assured him, that though it was not a new house, the flooring was perfectly safe. The Doctor started from his reverie like a person waked out of his sleep, but spoke not a word."—*Boswell's Life of Dr. Johnson, vol.* i. *p.* 76. In the same work other of his tricks are recorded, as talking to himself, measuring his steps in a mysterious manner, half whistling, clucking like a hen, rubbing his left knee, &c. Many sensible persons, with whom I am now acquainted, when particularly thoughtful, discover strange bodily motions, of which they are by no means conscious at the time.

[8] This gritty matter, subjected to chemical examination, was found to be *phosphat of lime.*

[9] This appearance I have found frequently to occur in maniacs who have suffered a violent paroxysm of considerable duration: and in such cases, when there has been an opportunity of inspecting the contents of the cranium after death, water has been found between the dura mater and tunica arachnoidea.

[10] Morbid Anatomy, page 304.

[11] Mr. Fourcroy does not appear to have given any particular attention to this fluid. He says, "Cette humeur ne

paraît pas différer de celle qui mouille toutes les parois membraneuses du corps humain en general, et dont j'ai déja parlé. C'est un liquide mucoso gelatineux, plus ou moins albumineux, et contenant *quelques matiéres salines.*"— *Systéme des Connoisances Chimiques,* 8vo. tom. ix. *p.* 303.

[12] It may be remarked, that all children in the early attempts at language, speak of themselves and others in the third person, and never employ the pronoun; they likewise never use connectives, or the inflections of verbs, until they begin to acquire some knowledge of numbers. Beyond this rude state our patient never advanced.

[13] For this term the indulgent reader must give the author credit, because he finds himself unable adequately to explain it.—It is a complex *term* for many ideas, on which language has not as yet, and perhaps will never be imposed. Very unfortunately there are many terms of this nature, equally incapable of description—a smile, for instance, is not very easy to be defined. Dr. Johnson calls it "a slight contraction of the face" which applies as properly to a paralytic affection. He also states it to be "opposed to frown." If curiosity should prompt the inquisitive reader to seek in the same author for the verb, to frown, he will find it "to express displeasure *by contracting the face* to wrinkles." He who would

"Finde the minde's construction in the face"

must not expect to be able to communicate to others, in a few words, that knowledge which has been the slow and progressive accumulation of years.

[14] These are the usual terms employed by writers on this subject, but the propriety of their use must be left to the judgment of the reader. Every person will occasionally

hesitate whether certain occurrences, said to be causes, ought to be referred to one class, in preference to the other. They are loose and vague names: for instance, a course of debauchery long persisted in, would probably terminate in paralysis; excessive grief we know to be capable of the same effect. Paralysis frequently induces derangement of mind, and in such case it would be said, that the madness was induced by the paralysis as a physical cause. But it often happens that debauchery and excessive grief are followed by madness, without the intervention paralysis. Moral, in this sense, means merely habitudes or customs, reiteration of circumstances confirmed into usage; and these may be indifferently accounted physical or moral.

[15]

"——nessun maggior dolore,
Che ricordarsi del tempo felice
Nella miseria."—*Dante*.

[16] The Jews also were particularly instrumental in the practice and propagation of medical knowledge at that period.

[17] Cogitatio, (hîc minimè prætereunda) est motus peculiaris Cerebri, quod hujus facultatis est proprium organum: vel potiùs Cerebri pars quædam, in medulla spinali et nervis cum suis meningibus continuata, tenet animi principatum, motumque perficit tam cogitationis quam sensationis; quæ secundùm Cerebri diversam in omnium animalium structuram, mirè variantur.—*Tolandi Pantheisticon, p.* 12.

[18] 1796, 1797.

[19] Vide Report, Part II. p. 25.

[20] Report, p. 59.

[21] Ibid, 57.

[22] Report 54.

[23] "We shall use the general term of methodism, to designate these three classes of fanatics, [Arminian and Calvinistic methodists, and the *evangelical* clergymen of the church of England] not troubling ourselves to point out the finer shades, and nicer discriminations of lunacy, but treating them all as in one general conspiracy against common sense, and rational orthodox christianity."—*Edinburgh Review, Jan. 1808, p. 342.*

[24] Traité Medico-Philosophique sur l'Alienation Mentale, 8vo. Paris, an. 9, p. 47.

[25] The late Reverend Dr. Willis.

[26] With respect to the persons, called Keepers, who are placed over the insane, public hospitals have generally very much the advantage. They are there better paid, which makes them more anxious to preserve their situations by attention and good behaviour: and thus they acquire some experience of the disease. But it is very different in the private receptacles for maniacs. They there procure them at a cheaper rate; they are taken from the plough, the loom, or the stable; and sometimes this tribe consists of decayed smugglers, broken excisemen, or discharged sheriffs' officers:

"All that at home no more can beg or steal."

How well such a description of persons is calculated to regulate and direct the conduct of an insane gentleman may be easily conjectured. If any thing could add to the calamity of mental derangement, it would be the mode which is generally adopted for its cure. Although an office of some importance and great responsibility, it is held as a degrading and odious employment, and seldom accepted but by idle and disorderly persons.

[27] Vide Cullen, First Lines, vol. iv. p. 154.

[28] *"D'uno luogo chiamato Timarahane, dove si castigano i matti.*

"In Costantinopoli fece fare un luogo Sultan Paiaxit dove si dovessero menare i pazzi, accioche non andassero per la citta, facendo pazzie, et è fatto à modo d'uno Spedale, dove sono circa cento cinquanta guardiani in loro custodia, et sonvi medicine, et altre cose per loro bisogni, e i detti guardiani vanno per la citta con bastoni cercando i matti, et quando ne truovano alcuno, lo'ncatenano per il collo con cathene di ferro, et per le mani, et à suon di bastoni lo menano al detto luogo, et quivi gli mettono una catena al collo assai maggiore, che è posta nel muro, et viene sopra del letto, tal mente che nel letto per il collo tutti gli tengono incatenati, et vene saranno per ordine, lontano l'uno dall'altro numero di quaranta, i quali per piacere di quelli della citta molte volte sono visitati, et di continovo col bastone i guardiani gli stanno appresso: Percio che non essendovi guastano i letti, et tiransi le tavole l'uno à l'altro: et venuta l'hora del mangiare, i guardiani gli vanno esaminando tutti per ordine, et trovando alcuno, che non istia in buon proposito, crudelmente lo battono, et se à caso truovano alcuno, che non faccia piu pazzie, gli banno miglior cura, che à gli altri." *J. Costumi et la vita de Turchi di Gio. Antonio Menavino Genovese da Vultri,* 12mo, *in Fiorenza,* 1551.

[29] Traité sur la Mania, page 103.

[30] The frequent recurrence of any propensity leads, by sure steps, to the final adjustment of the character; and even when the propensity is ideal, the repetition of the fits will, in the end, invest fancy with the habitudes of nature.—*Criticism on the Elegy written in a Country Church Yard, p.* 3.

[31] Remarks on Dr. Batties' Treatise on Madness, p. 38.

[32] Dr. Cox, Practical Observations on Insanity, p. 28.

[33] Dr. John Monro's Remarks on Dr. Battie, p. 39.

[34] Vide Dr. Cox's *Practical* Obs. on Insanity, p. 42.

[35] It is a painful recollection to recur to the number of interesting females I have seen, who, after having suffered a temporary disarrangement of mind, and undergone the brutal operation of *spouting*, in private receptacles for the insane, have been restored to their friends without a front tooth in either jaw. Unfortunately the task of forcing patients to take food or medicines is consigned to the rude hand of an ignorant and unfeeling servant: it should always be performed by the master or mistress of the mad-house, whose reputations ought to be responsible for the personal integrity of the unhappy beings committed to their care.

[36] Dr. Cox.

[37] See Dr. Cox's Advertisement prefixed to his book.

[38] Vide Report from the select committee appointed to enquire into the state of lunatics, page 25.

[39] Remarks on Dr. Batties' Treatise on Madness.

[40] See Dr. Cox, page 102.

[41] Dr. Cox, p. 61.

www.ingramcontent.com/pod-product-compliance
Lightning Source LLC
Chambersburg PA
CBHW070121260726
48658CB00001B/201